# Mediumship

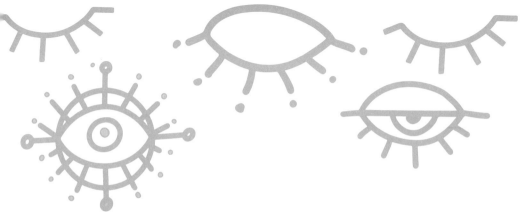

# Mediumship

Your guide to communicating and healing
through the spirit world

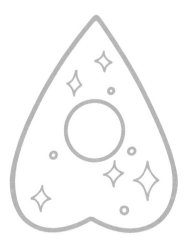

## Kerrie Erwin

ROCKPOOL

A Rockpool book
PO Box 252
Summer Hill
NSW 2130
Australia

rockpoolpublishing.co
Follow us! **f** 🅾 rockpoolpublishing
Tag your images with #rockpoolpublishing

ISBN: 9781925924985

Published in 2021 by Rockpool Publishing
Copyright text © Kerrie Erwin 2021
Copyright design © Rockpool Publishing 2021

Design and typesetting by Dana Brown, Rockpool Publishing
Edited by Lisa Macken

 A catalogue record for this
book is available from the
National Library of Australia

Printed and bound in China
10 9 8 7 6 5 4 3 2

From a performing arts background, Sydney-based international medium Kerrie Erwin has lived between two worlds since childhood and is able to see and hear spirit people talking. Realising her true calling when she was very young, she now works professionally as a spiritual medium and clairvoyant who focuses on spirit rescue, hauntings and connecting people to loved ones who have passed over into the spirit world. She has taught mediumship and metaphysics for many years, reads tarot cards and works with feng shui. She is also trained in spiritual hypnotherapies and past-life regression.

Kerrie regularly writes for magazines, works on radio and television, is the author of eight other books and regularly tours the Kerrie Erwin spiritual show. She works both locally in Australia and internationally via phone, Skype and other media.

www.pureview.com.au

*'Confirmation and validation of life after death can be an incredible comfort as it offers healing and evidence that our loved ones are safe after their passage into the spirit world. No matter how deep the grief, it can be lifted by the simple gift of love. Life as we know it is a roller coaster of incredible experiences but death is always the same, a passage to a new beginning.'*

– White Feather (my spirit guide)

*'The gift of prayer and faith is simple magic that connects us to the source of pure, unconditional love in our world. It is a direct line to the spirit world where we can receive guidance, healing, assistance and just about anything in life we need to help us move forward, from death of a loved one or inconsolable grief in its rawest form. Prayer is also a way to put out positive energy, to others less fortunate in life with hopeful, healing, mindful and loving thoughts. Christ-consciousness energy is the origin of the greatest source of positive and powerful unconditional love in the universe. It is part of something far greater than ourselves or what we could even imagine. God's loving energy inspires us to return that love and share it with others less fortunate than ourselves.'*

– White Feather

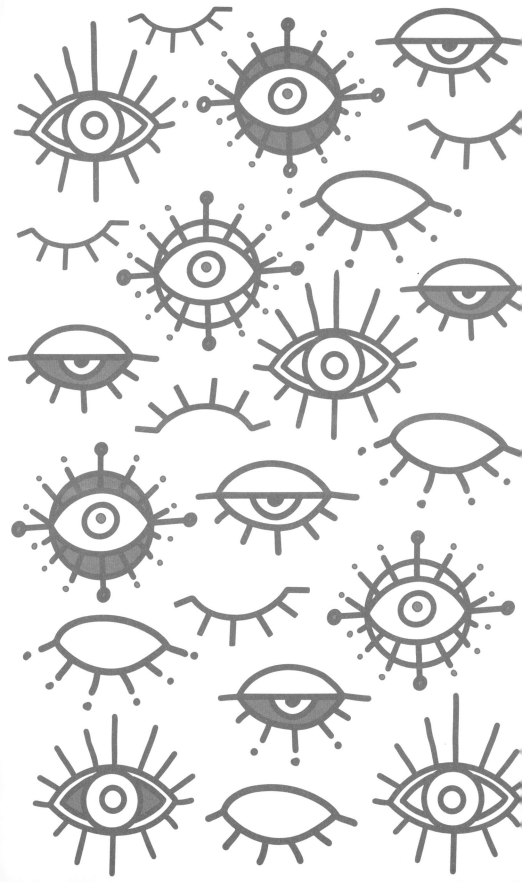

# CONTENTS

Preface: the miracle of love — 1

Introduction — 7

1. What is mediumship? — 19
   The difference between mediums and psychics — 22
   Opening your awareness — 24
   Using breath to prepare for mediumship — 25

2. Types of mediumship — 29
   Mental mediumship — 29
   Trance mediumship — 32
   Channelling — 40
   Transfiguration — 41
   Physical mediumship — 44
   Direct-voice mediumship — 52
   Spirit rescue (ghost busting) — 53
   Working with the police force — 57

3. Signs spirit is with us — 65

4. Suicide: a difficult subject — 75

5.  Gifts to work with: the clairs ............ 81

Clairvoyance: clear seeing ............ 82

Clairaudience: clear hearing ............ 82

Clairsentience: clear feeling ............ 83

Clairsalience: clear smelling ............ 83

Clairgustance: clear tasting ............ 84

Claircognizance: clear knowing ............ 85

Development exercises for your clairs ............ 85

6.  Spiritual churches ............ 97

Spiritual healing ............ 104

7.  Protection from negative energy ............ 107

Working with light energy ............ 108

Psychic attack ............ 112

Protecting your environment ............ 115

Protecting others from your negativity ............ 118

Protecting yourself from negativity ............ 118

Psychic thought forms ............ 121

White room exercise ............ 122

Cutting ties exercise ............ 124

8.  Boundaries ............ 127

9.  Meditation ............ 133

Creating an altar or sacred space for meditation ............ 134

Meditation for your higher self ............ 136

Meditation to clear your energy ............ 139

Group oversoul ............ 141

| 10. | The chakra system | 143 |
| | Visualising through the chakras | 147 |
| | Empowering with the middle pillar | 150 |
| | Closing down your chakras | 152 |
| 11. | Psychic links | 155 |
| | Linking in the classroom | 156 |
| | Linking through your aura | 157 |
| | Linking through numbers | 159 |
| | Double links | 161 |
| | Flower readings | 162 |
| | Jewellery readings | 164 |
| | Photograph readings | 166 |
| | Pendulums | 167 |
| | Ouija boards | 168 |
| | Automatic writing | 170 |
| | Distant healing | 172 |
| 12. | My spirit team | 175 |
| 13. | Ethics for professional mediums | 183 |
| | What clients can expect | 186 |
| Afterthought | | 189 |
| Recommended Reading | | 193 |

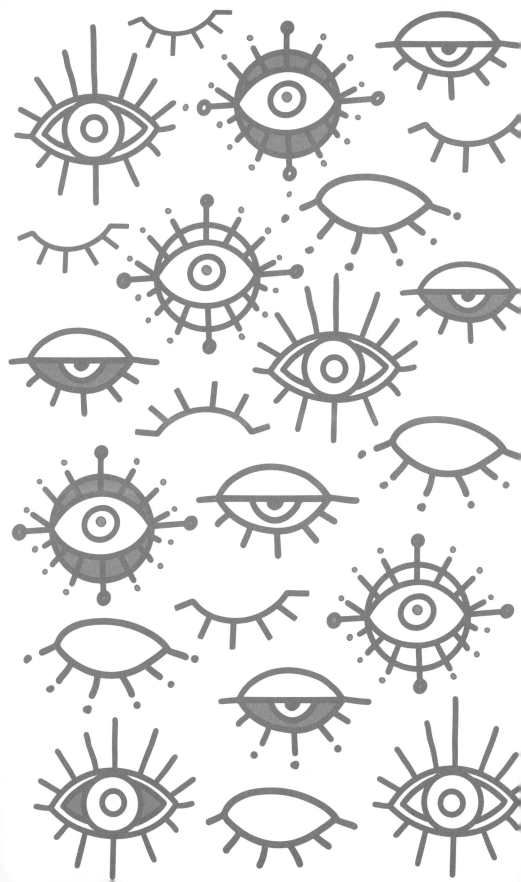

# PREFACE:

## The miracle of love

'Love comforteth like sunshine after rain.'
– William Shakespeare

Every Tuesday I would go for a walk with my great friend Soula. We always managed to have a good laugh while exercising, and would often share stories about our friends, our lives and whatever else was going on. Sometimes we'd have to stop from laughing so much, but it was a lot of fun and walking with a good friend is comforting for the soul. Exercise is very important for a medium as it is grounding and brings balance to your life as you take time out for yourself.

The work we do is incredibly demanding on so many levels. I don't know how many times I have felt deeply saddened and emotionally drained by the stories I've heard, but I have learned to use boundaries so it is no longer a problem. However, one day I listened to a message on my answering machine from a woman called Julie. She wanted me to help her find a medium in Queensland for her sister, as her niece had died. Even though I was tired and aching all over from the big workout with Soula, I decided to help Julie as I have always been fond of assisting children in any way I can. Survival evidence is the best way to do that. When I returned Julie's call I suddenly sensed a little girl in spirit standing next to me in the healing room of my home.

I said to Julie: 'I have a small girl here who is very persistent, telling me she wants to talk to her mummy. She is around seven years old, has light hair and is a bit of a chatterbox. She was sick for a long time and died in the hospital from cancer. Is this correct?'

'Yes, that's right,' she gasped, totally bewildered. 'Have you got her with you now?'

'Seems to be the case,' I answered, bemused at how fast the little girl had come in from the early morning. 'She has been hanging around me all day and told me all about herself, how she loves music and dancing, especially Madonna, and how she hates to wear shoes.'

Julie was silent for a moment, then she said she would tell her sister I had made contact with her daughter and get her sister to call me. I lit a candle, as I always do for spirit, and waited for the mother to ring. The little girl in spirit danced around the room and started to talk non-stop. She was the most determined spirit child I have ever witnessed in my working life as a medium!

When the woman from Queensland rang her daughter, Anna, started to give survival evidence and messages via me to her poor grieving mother. She was concerned about how grief stricken her mother was, and informed me there was going to be a new baby born. Her mother started to cry and began to tell me how hard the pain was of losing her seven-year-old daughter as she loved her so much; they were soul mates. I tried to pull myself together and told the woman Anna had said she was coming back to live another life on earth so her mother shouldn't worry. I informed the woman her daughter was from her own soul group and they would always be connected with love.

After talking to the woman for half an hour my energy started to get really flat and I was slowly losing the link with Anna. I couldn't believe my ears with what came next: 'I just wish I could find some way to contact her again, as I miss her so much.'

The woman was so mired in her grief she did not understand the miracle that was happening.

'I would like to help you understand what is going on here,' I gently replied. 'Your daughter in spirit has found a medium who lives in a different state from you but has got in contact with you to get her message of love across. That is proof of the miracle that love is eternal.' The woman began to cry again, but was able to understand that her brave daughter had found a way to make contact from the other side with her mother, which would help her mother on the road to healing she so greatly needed.

Anna's mother rang me on the one-year anniversary of Anna's death to say she was eight weeks pregnant, and asked if she could speak to her daughter. Almost immediately Anna came into the room, this time on a swing. Her hair was longer and she told me she always wanted to have long hair. She had grown in the spirit world and had come to pass on more information through her mother's love. They were both excited about the new baby. After an hour of speaking with both of them I was completely exhausted and said: 'I wouldn't be surprised if it is Anna who comes back as your next baby, but whatever happens I do know you will have a very healthy baby boy.' Anna's mum did give birth to a beautiful baby boy and was over the moon, as she had been told by her doctor it would be just about impossible to have any more children. She said her baby boy reminded her of Anna every time she looked deep into his eyes. She kept thinking it was her imagination, but they looked so familiar. Also, the boy had the same birthmarks on his body as Anna had had. The similarities were incredible, and when we discussed this over the phone I got goosebumps all over my body.

It's amazing how wonderfully spirit works. Situations such as these make you believe there truly are miracles in life.

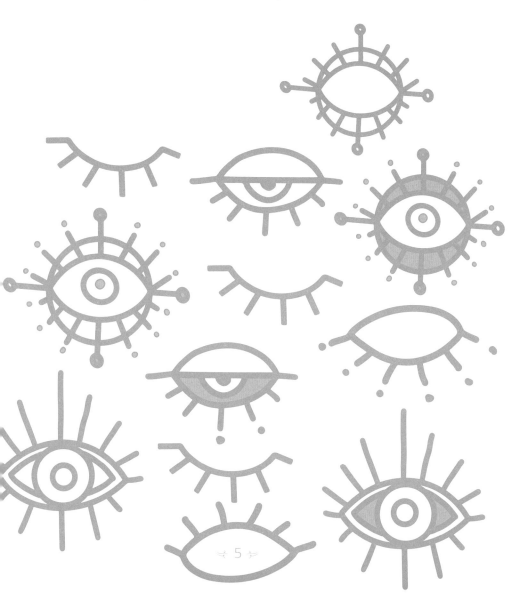

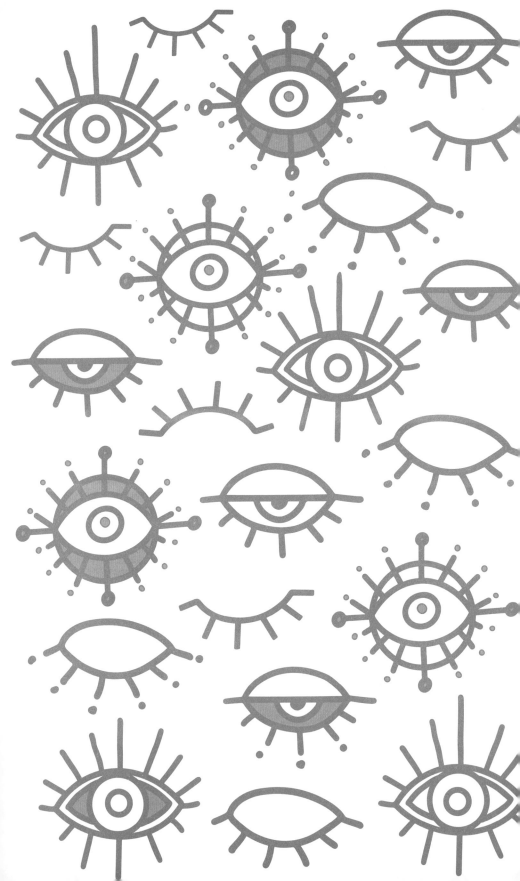

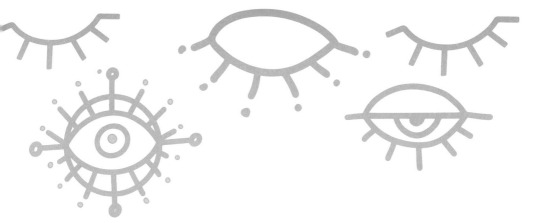

# INTRODUCTION

Love is the most powerful emotion in the world as its energy, in its higher form, can create healing, miracles and magic in our world. When a loved one dies there is no ending but rather a new beginning, a journey back to the spirit world as spirit lives on, connected to us eternally. There is no such thing as death; it's just a transition and journey into another dimension. Many people ask me what happens when you die, and what I know is this: your main guide from birth generally assists with your departure, and sometimes angels are involved if it is a child or a particularly tragic death. Once in the spirit world you are taken with your guide to the life review, to see how well you have done with all your spirit contracts while on earth. You go to the library where all the records of every life you have ever lived are stored then you are taken to rejoin your own spirit soul groups until it is time to reincarnate once again. Some souls may even spend time in a transitional phase or holding space – which acts as a spiritual hospital – for healing if the death was tragic.

I first started seeing and sensing spirit all around me when I was quite young, thinking it was normal. I also astral travelled all over the place and knew things about others I shouldn't have known about. Whenever I opened up and told anybody about my world and my experiences I would often be ridiculed and told to stop making up stories with my incredible imagination, as there was no one like me in the family and everybody had no idea what I was talking about. I soon learned that it would be best for everyone concerned to say nothing about my ghostly experiences and just try to fit in. I wanted to be normal and have a life where people liked me, so I kept my paranormal experiences a secret. I don't know how many times I got into trouble when I told Mum things I saw, such as the old man down the street who had died the week prior walking along the street or the woman around the corner walking her two dogs even though they had all died years ago. The only way to stop the spirit traffic visiting me in the dead of night was keeping on a night light. This deterred curious busy body spirits all trying to get my attention, as spirits are always drawn to my energy and prefer the dark as the light drains their energy. A sheet over my head helped too, but sometimes it got too hot in the summer months and was unbearable.

When I had a near-death experience in my early 20s I was thrust out of my body and taken with incredible speed out of this world and into a place of light, warmth and what I can only describe as all-encompassing, all-consuming loving oneness. It happened so fast, and before I could even think about anything I was back in my body and my friend was hysterically screaming out my name in my face as I lay on the ground, confused and aching like hell, while my whole body shook. Years later a hypnotherapist explained I had been in the spirit world, just an arm's length away from our own reality.

After years of learning and working as a spiritualist and due to my own curiosity I have visited the spirit world many times via dreams, meditation and hypnotherapy, and it is always the same. It is a place you can only imagine, a vast consciousness of light and warmth where nobody has any problems, everything is love and everywhere you look there is nothing but lightness, bright vivid colours and not one hint of darkness. It's a different experience for everybody – some people may see buildings or cities, others clouds or nature – but it is always a place where love governs supreme.

I have been told by different spirit people that they are no longer suffering from however they died, as they left the old body behind and are now in a spirit body with a consciousness and intelligence. Spirit people appear to be in their prime and, although they no longer need food, they still talk about earthly pleasures such as their favourite foods and other small comforts they loved while alive, which provides evidence for the loved ones left behind. One young man who came through had been decapitated but he talked enthusiastically about how he loved his bike so much he wanted to sleep next to it in his room. His girlfriend laughed when I told her this and said she used to think he cared more about the bike than about her.

Women spirits often talk about family and children (if the children are having problems) and their gardens. I've also had spirit people come through giving strict instructions on what they want their loved ones to do with their belongings. The mother of two sisters who consulted me came through, and all she talked about was selling her property for a good price as it had been her life's investment. The sisters were so stunned to hear this, but they stopped crying and took note of their mother's instructions as she had died suddenly on an operating table and they didn't know what her final wishes were.

If and when a spirit person wants to get a message across they will leave no stone unturned to do so. It's amusing to hear these stories because people's personalities when you connect to them in the spirit world don't change: they are usually the same as when they had been living. Often when a spirit person communicates the first thing they tell me is how they died followed by things peculiar to their lives, as evidence for their loved ones. This has taught me repeatedly there are no secrets in the spirit world.

Happily, I have witnessed many times in my readings that when children die they generally talk about coming back into the family again and will often return to the same families or soul groups. Pets can also return to the same family. One lady told me she would swear her new stray cat was her deceased horse as the cat seemed so familiar; they had the same personality. The lady had an overwhelming feeling of pure love and was overjoyed the horse was back with her in her life, as its departure had been very painful.

A child lost through miscarriage will often come back as the same soul, which can be identified and confirmed by a birthmark, a knowing or just by looking into the child's eyes. Children who don't return stay in the spirit world by choice, as life on earth can be quite harsh, with many trials and tribulations. It is a great comfort to people to know this simple reality. If a son comes back as a daughter I can still make contact with the daughter because, even though the soul reincarnates, a part of the soul remains in the spirit world.

With a tragic death such as suicide, car accident, murder, being burnt in a fire or drowning the spirit will generally come out of the body before the impact so they never suffer. My guides have advised me repeatedly over the years that a soul instinctively knows when it is going to die from the incident. My sister lost a friend in the horrendous 2019/2020 Australian bush fires. The friend, a farmer and a beautifully strong, independent woman who loved all her animals, perished when she returned home to rescue her cat. When I made a connection with her spirit she laughed and told me to reassure my sister she never suffered as she flew out of her body when the fumes and smoke knocked her out.

In my younger years I worked as a nursing sister, and when a patient was dying all their relatives in spirit would gather around singing songs, playing a piano or talking around the bed. I used to shake my head with disbelief and think: is there a party going on? I also know our loved ones in spirit like to go to their own funerals. The first time it happened I saw my cousin, Jan, standing by her coffin. She looked beautiful and was dressed in a white gown like an angel and there was no evidence of the thin, emaciated, cancer-ravaged body she died with. I have seen this phenomenon many times at other funerals with friends and relatives and have heard in many readings the spirit describe the whole event, what song was played and what went on in great detail, which is incredible when you think about it.

In the private séances I run Johnny the spirit boy will often say the spirit of Paul Walker (from the *Fast & Furious* movie franchise) dropped him and the spirit children off in his fast car, or other spirit people will say they have all the relatives in the back of the old car they used to drive when they were alive. Over the years my work for spirit as a medium has reinforced the fact that the more devotion and time I put into my work the more I learn, just as with everything in life you put time and effort into. The spirit world is an amazing place of discovery as you are constantly learning new things and helping people along the way. Once you get on the path spirit will lead you along and teach you many things. Everybody will have their own way of learning and experience different things.

I was taught in my early training that natural mediums have a light around their aura that generates a lighthouse-like beacon to visiting spirits and souls lost in the grey world of the astral. Once I learned how to close my energy centres down I was safe and able to live a normal life. I used to have an invisible friend, a spirit elderly man with a strong English accent. I had long conversations with him, and whenever Mum angrily asked me who I was talking to I wouldn't tell her as it was my secret and she probably would not have believed me anyway. I found out later through my father that the elderly man was probably my grandfather, who died when I was a baby. My spirit friend disappeared when I started Sunday school, which I loved as the whole room would light up with loving energy and hundreds of angels. I also loved Bible stories about Jesus, a natural medium and healer who worked with angels. As I grew older I felt safe and thought it was time to tell everyone my secret, so I naively told a visiting evangelist who seemed like a lovely woman. However, when I told her I was able to see and hear spirits talking or know things that were going to happen she totally freaked out. My trust in the woman was unwarranted and people began to look at me with fear in their eyes. I was asked to leave the church.

The persecution I often experienced was overwhelmingly sad for me, as I felt as though I had finally found a home to fit in and for a while it was such a good feeling. It was one of my life's lessons: that people are often not who they say they are. People don't change, but we do have freedom in how we want to live our lives. These days I have learned to walk away from the hurt and sadness, as it's easier. I send judgemental people love and wish them well. You can't make people love or respect you or have relationships with people who don't understand what you are all about, because it makes you ill and you will not often know why people behave in terrible ways. I use healing modalities such as spiritual healing, reiki, natural therapies, past-life regression and hypnotherapy to improve my spiritual growth and to help people in any way I can as an energy and light worker.

As I have worked on myself over the years I've moved away from toxic people who are not on my wavelength, as not everybody who does this work is spiritual and I have met some very unpleasant types who are quite bluntly not spiritual but quite unpleasant and disingenuous. For this reason it is mandatory to use boundaries and protection every day. As a spiritual medium my aim is to work at my highest capacity, so I have studied with many gifted teachers from all over the world throughout my life. The best learning for me is through meditation, séances and dreams and working with my own spirit team, as I am constantly shown new things by my guides and angel helpers. My belief is that everything you learn in life is never wasted, as spirit will use what you have to spread the love of spirit and assist people through hard and difficult times.

I am a trance and practising psychical medium, which took years to develop but has been an extraordinary experience for my loyal sitters and myself as it teaches so much about the spirit world. I have also been involved in the location of missing persons. I only work with my guides, who are my teachers, most often through meditation, prayer, feelings, pictures in my mind or an inner voice, which is my higher self that constantly tells me things and gives me the information I need.

When you start to trust spirit and the way it all works you will always be looked after. One of my good friends and wise old teachers, Joan, who is now in the spirit world, always used to say that when you surrender and have faith spirit you will always have food on your table, a safe roof over your head and a good partner who loves you. These days when working for clients on the phone or in my presentations, as soon as I open up I will hear the spirit person talking in my ear as though it's a telephone connection, giving me proof of how they died, what they looked like, what sort of person they were and names and places. Once the spirit has settled I will often have long conversations as they like to go into great detail about what my client has been up to. It never ceases to amaze me how the spirit person always knows everything that has been going on in my clients' lives. Spirit communication is a wonderful healing tool for the grief process, as it is evidence the soul lives on and we are eternally connected to their undying love.

I wrote this book to encourage others like myself to follow their calling and embrace the gifts they have been given. The earth experience is a stage, and we are here to learn from all that happens to us and help everyone in whatever ways we can.

**_Love, light and blessings . . ._**

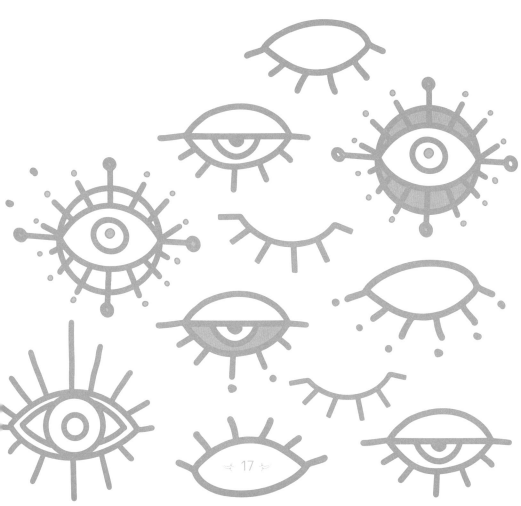

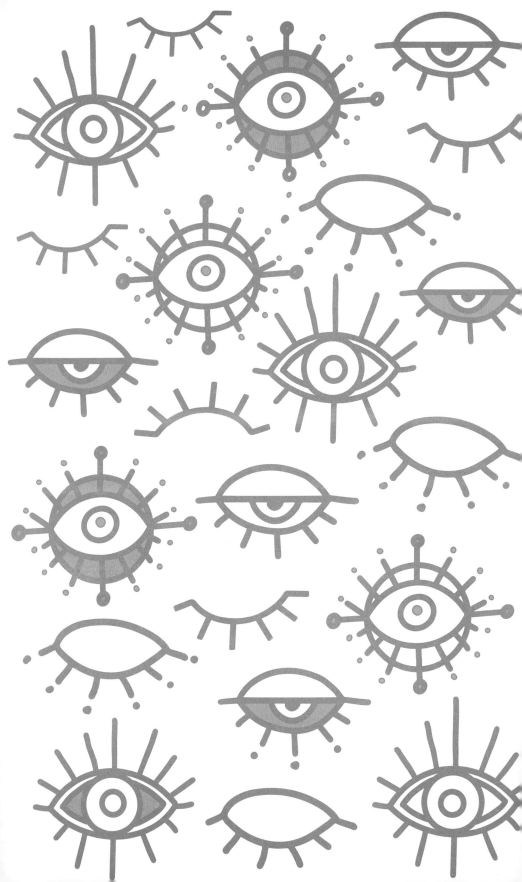

# CHAPTER 1

# What is mediumship?

Mediumship is the practice of mediating communication between living humans and the spirits of the dead. It has been documented from early human history, gaining its popularity during the nineteenth century when Ouija boards were used by the upper classes as a source of entertainment. Natural mediums are born with the gift, although they may not become aware of it until later in life. Every person who walks this path has their own individual gift to offer. Once you embrace mediumship as your life purpose it becomes an enormous responsibility, as you are helping people to cope with their grief. Despite the highs and lows it is very rewarding.

I became aware of my gift from a very young age, but I know other excellent well-trained mediums who have woken up to their gifts through deep trauma, a near-death experience, illness, an accident, a life-changing occurrence or the death of a loved one. I tried to switch my gift off for many years as I felt that I never wanted to be a medium and got into trouble from family members if I spoke about my visions, but spirit was always persistent and drew me back all the time.

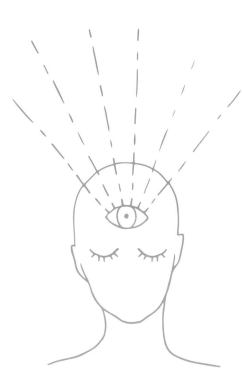

I didn't undertake full-time training until I was in my thirties, when I realised I would never make it as an actor. Everything was full on for a while as I'd been suppressing my gifts for years, but it did finally settle down. Once you work with spirit it is always with you no matter what you do to suppress it, as it is part of who you are as a soul and part of your spiritual purpose.

My gifts have been with me since birth. In my early twenties I was newly married and on a holiday in Norway. My husband and I were staying at his grandfather's old cabin in the woods when an angry spirit man with a snarl on his face tried to strangle me in the middle of the night in my sleep. It was horrifying, because while my husband was snoring next to me in the bed the spirit was trying to suffocate me. I felt a heaviness on my body that made it impossible to breathe. After saying the Lord's prayer the sinister thing disappeared, but I remember lying awake all night because I was so terrified. In the morning I noticed there was a photo on the wall of the same man who had been in my dream and asked my husband who it was; it was his grandfather.

It seemed to me as though it had been a warning to stay away, and as it turned out the marriage was very short and ended badly because of domestic violence. I am sure if I confessed my experience to anybody they would have told me I was mad. I still remember my nursing days and how amazing it was to see spirit people in a room when somebody was going to die all gathered at the end of the patient's bed. Sometimes the patient would say they could see their mother or father around them, but the nurses thought they were delusional.

A very good friend of mine went through a terrible series of events that saw the deaths of her young husband, mother and father very close together. She had a young child and was very depressed, but spirit stepped in because her mother in spirit, looking like she was in her thirties, visited her one day and told her to wake up to herself as she was sick of seeing her daughter this way. My incredulous friend thankfully realised this was a spirit intervention, and everyone was relieved when she pulled herself together and turned her life around. All the grief and sadness she had been carrying slowly healed, and she married a few years later and had more children. The power of love saved her and helped put her back on her feet again. After spending time with some teachers for her own development, she is now a successful medium who often has her deceased family members helping her with her stage work. Like myself, she helps many people understand that there really is no such thing as death; it's merely a transformation to another place, the spirit world. We are eternally connected to our loved ones through the power of love.

## THE DIFFERENCE BETWEEN MEDIUMS AND PSYCHICS

Most people have some psychic abilities, because at its simplest it means using your natural intuition or trusting your innate feelings.  Nine times out of ten your gut will be correct and help you make decisions in particular situations. A professional *psychic* uses ESP to identify information about a person's past, present or future via clairvoyance or telepathy. They have worked on their gifts or had some training, and can be extremely talented and have very helpful insights, advice and counsel.

As with all forms of spiritual abilities you can learn to be a psychic, but *mediums* are born with a natural ability although, as mentioned, they may not know they have the ability until later in life. All mediums are psychic, but not all psychics are mediums and often won't be able to make contact with the spirits of departed loved ones or give specific information that indicates they are linking with a particular individual as they don't have that ability. A medium has the right spirit team, clears the energy the first time they meet with a client and uses a psychic link to get in contact with a spirit.

## OPENING YOUR AWARENESS

Here is a simple five-day 'living in the present' activity to help you open your awareness for your spiritual journey. Don't mix the exercises; keep each one for a separate day.

You will be surprised how much this simple practice opens you up and, over time, makes you more sensitive and aware of the energy around you. The world is an interesting place, and the presence of things you never really saw before will reveal themselves in a much bigger way. Because of our busy lives we forget to daydream or live simply in the *now*.

**Day 1:** lie down or sit quietly for a couple of moments and identify as many different sounds as possible. Also, be open during the day to identifying different noises that you hear. This will open up the chakras in your ears and will help if you want to develop your clairaudience (clear hearing).

**Day 2:** look at the ceiling and the walls of wherever you are. Identify as many colours as possible and, during your day, stop and look at them again. This will help you open up to seeing different colours in people's energy fields.

**Day 3:** become aware of different smells. Do not be judgemental;

just acknowledge they exist. This awareness will develop the more you practise and will help you in your mediumship to indentify the scents surrounding loves ones in spirit.

**Day 4:** open up your senses and become aware of touch and texture: smooth or rough, cold or hot and so on.

**Day 5:** become aware of taste and of all the ingredients. Try eating different foods to develop this awareness.

## USING BREATH TO PREPARE FOR MEDIUMSHIP

One of the greatest types of healing in the world in my opinion is linking with our loved ones in the spirit world. To be able to make contact with and provide evidence our loved ones are safe and secure in the afterlife is very powerful and proves time and time again that love is the most potent type of energy in the universe and is eternal.

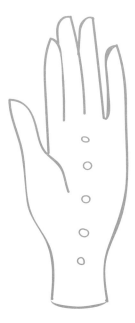

The following exercise will help you to prepare for working as a medium. It will not only assist you to become more receptive in your work, but with practice will help you grow and become more proficient.

- Find a place where you won't be disturbed and sit up nice and straight so all your chakras are in alignment.
- Close your eyes and take a few deep, gentle breaths in and out. Repeat three times. Release any mind clutter and feel your body starting to relax.
- Starting with your toes, tense the muscles then relax them. Do the same with your ankles.
- Gradually begin to work all the way up the body. Pay attention to your solar plexus, and release any emotion you may be holding there. Finish with the eyes and the muscles of the face.
- Bring energy up from the earth star to the base of your spine. Try to feel a gentle heat or a shift in energy as this chakra opens.
- Using your breath, take the power slowly all the way up to the crown chakra, then let it cascade like a fountain of light down through all the centres and through your entire body, filling it with vitality.
- You have drawn up earth energy, now draw down the spiritual energy of the higher realms into your crown centre.

- Let a ball of gold light descend to all of the chakras in turn.
- Feel the love. Know now that this energy will not only help you, it will also protect and shield you against psychic and physical negativity.
- Feel the streams of energy merging at your heart centre. Your heart is the point of balance, and everything that happens now will be motivated by love.
- Hold your attention on your heart as your loved ones in spirit are connected to this love. Send your thoughts out to the spirit world, asking them to blend their energies and work with you today.

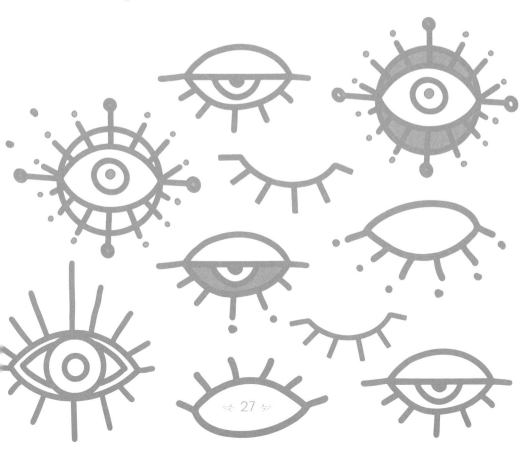

# CHAPTER 2

# Types of mediumship

We now know what a medium is, but what are their gifts and different abilities and exactly how do they communicate with spirit? In this chapter I outline the different aspects of mediumship and the work of mediums with the paranormal in greater detail.

## MENTAL MEDIUMSHIP

I work mainly as a mental medium. I have my own style, never copy anyone and never take anything for granted as circumstances change all the time. From my early thirties, spirit had me working non-stop on platforms and in stage shows with big audiences, as I was trained to entertain. Never in a million years did I think I would end up being a stage medium, as my dream was to be an actor. I worked very hard and spent a long time studying and practising my craft, as you are always learning new things and having different experiences. I want to work at my highest potential, as it is my 'soul' purpose to help people and make a difference in the world.

In my early days of training I was told every person has four methods or channels for receiving divine guidance and messages from their higher self, spirit helpers, guides and angels through the senses: sight, sound, smell and feelings/thought. As you work more on yourself as a light worker, not only will you become more sensitive and be attracted to others like yourself, but spirit will increase these channels and your vibration will lift and take you to a much higher vibration. My best gift is clear healing, or clairaudience, as I am able to hear the spirit person talking in my ear as if on a telephone. I have to listen carefully then all the other senses kick in, so it's no surprise that the majority of my work is phone readings because all I have to do is sit back and repeat the voice I am hearing in my ear.

For my stage work I work with my guide, Romanov, who stands on my left side. He lines all the spirits up in a queue so they don't jump in when I'm working, which helps to make the connection clearer. Before I work on a stage I also get all the spirits' names as they come in for the night. I write them down on a piece of paper and call them out on the day. I also get random spirits, or people ask questions and I bring their loved one in. Sometime I will get what is called a 'double link'. If this happens I ask the spirits to separate and then read two or three spirits at a time. For example, I might have three Johns who suicided: a young John, a man in his thirties and a man in his fifties. I can generally feel what spirit I am with as I feel a pull, then I go to the relevant person and do the reading. In my early days I was able to see spirit walking around but there was too much spirit traffic. These days they come into my mind like a small picture or movie where I can see the person very clearly. Also in my early days as a medium I was able to hear animals and people's thoughts, which could be unpleasant. This happened out of the blue when I had my second child and was an awful experience, so I asked spirit to take it away because I need to be able to have a normal life and did not want to be bombarded with voices in my head.

Some famous mental mediums are Doris Stokes, James Van Praagh (television personality who describes himself as a clairvoyant and spiritual medium. He has written numerous books, including The New York Times bestseller Talking to Heaven), John Edward, Theresa Caputo, John Holland and Rita Rogers.

## TRANCE MEDIUMSHIP

*'Trance occurs when, through the induction of an altered state of consciousness, we allow the spirit world to "capture our attention" or even place a "hold" on our minds, enabling a closer blending with the spirit world. The degree of "hold" on the medium's mind will determine the quality and depth of trance.'*

– Arthur Findlay College

Trance is a very refined aspect of mediumship that influences our spirituality and our messages in mediumship. The blending of energy between spirit control and medium can be so strong that the medium can lose awareness without falling asleep. The process of trance occurs when we subdue our conscious minds and slow down our thinking, so the spirit world can impinge their minds on ours in order to establish their presence. In this state we can be in touch and at one with minds that influence, educate, uplift and inspire. In order to achieve the trance state, we must withdraw our awareness from the here and now and move our minds into an aspect of stillness. Then, losing our awareness/consciousness so we become subdued and passive, the spirit world moves closer and closer to the medium until they come to the fore of the medium's mind. In that stillness of mind is an inner knowing that keeps our minds out of the way.

Trance is *mental* mediumship, not physical; it's a process of mind connecting with mind. When we understand how the spirit controls impinge thoughts on the medium's mind, the greater the co-operation between the medium and spirit and the more control they have  When you achieve trance it's because you have got out of the way of your own thinking and allowed a collective mind to blend with yours and take control of your thinking processes. When the blending between spirit and medium is very close through many years of co-operation on both sides the spirit world almost takes over the medium's mind (with their consent) and their motor control,  making it possible to move around and demonstrating the trust between medium and spirit. This special relationship helps to build closer rapport and can bring a sharper, more specific and accurate flow of information in all areas of healing, mediumship, philosophy and teaching.

The following is a description of the levels of trance mediumship, as outlined by the Arthur Findlay College.

*Beginner:* there would be an achieved attunement/blending with spirit energy and ability to be inspired from one's own spirit and/or spirit discarnate. The medium would be capable of achieving an altered state of consciousness or subdued consciousness, working with external thought processes and giving spirit voice at a minimum. Light control would be evidence, taking inspiration further and achieving a deeper blending.

*Intermediate:* there would be a strong influence of spirit upon the medium's mind. The medium would be capable of achieving an altered state of consciousness, and blending with a discarnate personality would be evident. The spirit control would be able to speak through the medium for a short period of time. Onlookers would witness the spirit control objectively or subjectively through their clairvoyant vision or by sensing atmospheric changes clairsentiently.

*Advanced:* full spirit control of the medium's mind takes place. The medium would be in a state of mental 'hold' by spirit in an altered state of consciousness and have no recollection of proceedings. Information voiced will be fluent, intelligent, logical and rational, as well as uplifting and enlightening. Information achieved through trance mediumship should demonstrate a living intelligence extraneous to the medium's own understanding. An altered state of consciousness occurs when the ego is dissolved and there is a union with a formless, universal energy.

I have experienced intermediate trance for many years both by myself and with groups of like-minded people Most of my training was through a spiritual church in Australia throughout my life as a practising medium. Trance mediumship is like a deep meditation, but sometimes I don't remember everything that happens. If you want to be proficient at it and get results the only way is to have good, clear contact with your guides, who are our true spiritual teachers from the time we are born. We may have various guides who come and go throughout our development, but our main guide/s remain with us forever.

Trance mediumship is different to channelling as it is a deeper state of consciousness and sometimes it is hard to remember everything that occurred while in trance. When you speak to an entity or enlightened being that is being trance channelled you are speaking directly to that entity without the channel's personality acting as an intermediary or translator and there is less distortion of any information that you may receive. The experience is like having an interactive conversation with a wise and loving friend. One minister at a spiritual church often used a blue light when the room was darkened, which was very effective as it seemed to calm everything and made it easier to channel light beings, angels, master energies and spiritual guides. I have worked with animals as well, which have a soul, consciousness and a chakra system. I have also been able to channel many star people, which proves to me this is a huge universe and we are all one.

The first time I learned to trance was an incredible experience. I was sitting in a circle in a darkened room with three other mediums. A highly qualified teacher was leading the group and we were sitting close to each other, surrounded by a beautiful energy of light that our leader had set up. Relaxing with my eyes closed and paying special attention to my breath, I was suddenly overshadowed by a big loving male energy. Never in my life had I felt such a strong connection to anyone; there was so much love being directed to me all at once and I felt overwhelmed. My guide's energy was so enormous and strong it felt as if somebody really big was sitting on top of me. After I asked my guide to move aside I felt a lot better, as any fears I had just disappeared. Tears of happiness filled my eyes with the love I was feeling and the deep connection taking place with this being and me. My guide told me he was an Indian chief known as White Feather. He called himself 'Father' and showed me pictures in my mind's eye of the life we had lived together as father and son. This did not surprise me, as I have always had an affinity with indigenous people and especially native American Indians. I had the urge to play an imaginary drum that sat in my lap and went with the gentle flow that was happening.

I felt as though I was being teleported to another time and place where everything was simple, easy and free. At the same time my mind was in overdrive about my breakthrough and I wanted to learn everything there was to know. The energy quickly changed, though, as I began to hear a funny noise coming from the other side of the room. Even though I opened my eyes as my curiosity got the better of me I was able to stay in the energy, because some entities you channel come through when your eyes are open and others when they are closed. I almost burst out laughing at the sight of my friend Lorry, who was crawling around on her stomach like a big caterpillar or worm and making strange noises. This sudden change in energy and my laughter brought me straight back into my body. The teacher, realising the energy had shifted, decided to bring us all back into the room and close the circle. Our first lesson was over.

I have since discovered that some people may take longer to make a connection to their guide. They may even just fall asleep and think they are channelling, but you will know by their snoring that this is not the case. Some people vomit and make loud horrible noises while tapping their legs or hands when they first begin to work with the energy, or they walk around or dance. With one of my Indian guides I feel like I am riding a horse bareback over the plains. My whole body rocks and it must look a sight for others to see. Some people may even feel a very heavy energy in their throats and feel as though they are choking. Everyone is different and no one ever has the same experience, as this is all part of the journey in their teaching with spirit. I now prefer to work solo and run my own group, but when I go through change I will get together with other like-minded people as the group energy is usually a lot stronger. It is also important to have a good teacher or leader and someone experienced enough to know what they are doing. This energy work will take you to higher levels, as it is very uplifting.

I decided long ago not to work in a deep trance state as I don't like being completely overshadowed or forgetting everything. Not everyone can do deep trance work as it does take a lot of time and energy, and nobody should feel they have to do it or be forced. I once witnessed a young man being forced to go into a deep trance, but he was terrified each time he did it and would scream and shout before going into the state. When he awoke and came back into the room he could not recall anything that happened. This did not feel right to me as I felt the young man was not ready to do this type of work in his development. Shortly after this my guide, White Feather, advised me that perhaps it was time for me to move on from this group; I had continued there to get a better connection with my writing guide, Leon, who usually stayed in the background as I always had so many healing guides around me because of all the previous work I had been doing. Once I learned to ask the others to step back Leon stepped forward more, and my mediumship guide Romanov came forward. My writing became stronger and my mediumship went to new heights, which was quite an interesting experience. If you are meant to do something spirit will make it happen for you no matter what.

Whenever I want to speak to my guides all I have to do is gently close my eyes, and my loving and wise friends will always appear. All you need to do yourself is find a good teacher and sit with a like-minded group. It may take a while to get there but it is worth it in the end to learn who all your guides are and for them to come in and talk to you or through you. If anyone ever asks you who you are talking with you will be able to tell them precisely who the being is that is giving you your information. I can say that trance meditation or mediumship will be an integral part of your development as a serious psychic, medium or healer.

## CHANNELLING

Channelling is a beautiful and natural light form of communication between non-physical entities, animals, birds and all living things. It is not trance and it is safe, but I advise people to always close down after a session by imagining all their chakras or energy centres closing down like little lights. I have channelled nature spirits and found this very entertaining, especially little undine or water spirits. One of the guides I channel is a tiny water fairy called Erin. As we channel we allow ourselves to be an interpreter of the information we are getting. This is quite an easy process, because once you find a quiet place all you have to do is close your eyes and the flow of non-verbal information and communication will begin. I have received a lot of information this way, by lighting a candle, praying and receiving information from the angelic kingdom or ascended masters.

As we are all made up of consciousness it is possible to channel animals. I have channelled almost everything that is living, as living things have intelligence, a consciousness and compassion. Not long after I channelled my first cat, a stray cat landed on my doorstep. I adopted him, as he had nowhere else to go and had no intention of leaving anyway; I feel it was spirit's way of letting me know I had a new member for our family. I once sat with a girl who only channelled angels and a friend of mine often channels trees or plants, which as living beings have a soul. Animals have living souls as they too have a circle of life and incarnate as humans do, but we have a higher vibration than animals. Animals incur karma just the same way humans do, because for every action there is a reaction.

It may come as a surprise to learn that some animals incarnate specifically to be companions to certain souls. How many times have you seen an animal or pet that is highly intelligent, just like a human? Every living species on earth is connected to the divine source of love and has its own intelligence. As we evolve as humans and learn to raise our vibration we become more open to other concepts; as souls we continually learn lessons of tolerance.

## TRANSFIGURATION

The very first time I saw an incidence of transfiguration I was in a private sitting with a very talented medium in a spiritual church that was teaching us trance mediumship. As the medium went under in a trance state I was mightily amazed to see another person's face on top of hers. As she spoke to the person in the group we all gasped, as her face had become that of a man.

In fact, it was the deceased father of one of the sitters. Once the message was delivered the medium's face contorted and returned to normal, and she slowly came back into the room. Every one of us had tears in our eyes as it had been so moving, sad and emotional.

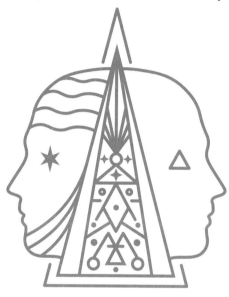

Another time I was in a church service when my talented teacher decided to trance on the platform without assistance. Straight away a strange woman's face appeared on top of hers and began giving messages.

As she had nobody to assist her my teacher had trouble coming out of the trance state, so I stepped up on the stage and called her back gently; it can be dangerous to touch somebody in this state.

She had gone very deep, and it was a while before she was aware and came back completely into her body. When I asked her what had happened she said very gruffly that the spirit that came into her body was too strong and she could not shift her. I have never seen this before or experienced it myself but it taught me to always have somebody with you when you are doing trance work.

As for other mediums, a transfiguration medium has the ability to communicate with those in the spirit world. It is about blending your vibrations and energy with the spirit in question to forge the connection. According to internationally renowned psychic medium, spiritual teacher, author and radio host John Holland, the medium enters a trance-like state or an altered state of consciousness. When the time is right a veil of ectoplasm slowly appears in front of their face that gets moulded into the exact features of the spirit who's trying to communicate. (Ectoplasm is a translucent substance that oozes from the medium's body during the trance state.) Spirits are able to manipulate and use the substance to push their own faces through the veil just like a mask. Once spirits have finished communicating, the ectoplasm returns to the medium's body. The substance is very light sensitive, which is why many transfiguration mediums hold séances in darkened rooms.

Transfiguration was very popular in the United Kingdom during the late 19th and early 20th centuries, when interest in spiritualism was at an all-time high as a result of the horrific aftermath of and human loss resulting from World War I. Thousands of people became interested in the reality of the afterlife. Grieving families tried to come to terms with the loss, often spanning generations as fathers, husbands and sons were lost during the war. Many people with heavy broken hearts wanted to know if there really was an afterlife and if their loved ones were safe. I found it immensely poignant to read about people who'd lost loved ones in the war who attended transfiguration séances in the hopes of seeing their loved ones' faces just one more time.

All too often when someone dies tragically their family members who are left to grieve have a harder time coming to terms with their loss, as they don't get the opportunity to say goodbye. I do want to reiterate, however, that this form of mediumship is quite rare. It takes absolute dedication and desire as well as patience to sit in a circle for years to develop the special ability.

## PHYSICAL MEDIUMSHIP

Physical mediumship is the process whereby a loved one in spirit or a spirit guide is able to physically manifest within our world via a medium. Most physical mediumship is presented in a darkened or dimly lit room; I often use a red light, which encourages spirit activity in the room. Physical mediums make use of a traditional array of tools and appurtenances including spirit trumpets, spirit cabinets and levitation tables. Physical mediumship can also produce the materialisation of apports, the paranormal transference of an article from one place to another or an appearance of an article from an unknown source that is often associated with spiritualistic séances. Materialised objects can range from flowers, jewellery, crystals, stones and shells. The production of apports is one of the most prominent and effective aspects of séances, with their behaviour varying from flying through the air, to hitting sitters in their faces to landing on the table or in people's laps. A favourite thing is to scatter perfume over the audience, which is quite incredible when it happens, or produce cool air.

Over the years I have had only one apport in my experimental séance work, which was a large stone that hit one of the sitters in the room on her head. It came flying through the air from the room next door, where it used to sit near the window. I was so pleased this had happened but unfortunately it never happened again, no matter how much I tried or asked spirit people to create it. We regularly have other effects such as knocking, voices, rapping, small tables spinning and rocking without help, cones being lifted and disappearing, lights coming on or flashing, bells ringing, orbs appearing, hot air, cold air, and spirits and children walking around the room by using ectoplasm created from the cells of the medium and sometimes the séance attendees. Transfigurations of different spirits over the medium have also occurred when I have brought loved ones of the sitters into the room. With the more experienced psychical mediums you can often see materialised body parts such as heads, hands or feet.

Unlike some mediums I never use 'human batteries', wherein the medium draws on other people's energy by getting them all to hold the medium's body parts. I personally find this distasteful as I like my sitters to be present and enjoy the experience. During the séance the medium goes into a light or deep trance depending on what the spiritual agreement is with the guide. When I first started going under in my private sittings I let my own main guide, White Feather, know I had no interest in going into deep trance states. Since I made that arrangement nothing has changed and I always have a good idea of most of the things that have happened in the session through the spirits that overshadowed me and spoke through me.

Through my séance experiments over 15 years I feel I am still just a novice, as it takes a lot of patience and years of regular sittings. It is always a learning experience, though, every time I do it. One good thing is that I have been able to heal sitters in the room with the advice of some of the spirit doctors I have brought through who lived in other centuries. One woman had to have an eye operation but with the healing energies it slowly recovered by itself. I have worked with many spirit doctors and highly evolved beings as they come and go. The spirit doctors always say after a healing to use white sheets on your bed, and to call them in so they can continue working on you while you sleep. They have also said to call them in whenever assistance is needed. Many of my sitters have related to me how things have gone after the session and how their illness improved and certain parts of their bodies were healed.

In my private sitting I have a young spirit boy called Johnny, who together with other spirit children brings in different entities as spirit operator in a safe environment. I first came into contact with Johnny when I was doing spirit shows called the rainbow show and sending money to a children's hospital. He came to me in a séance one night with five other delightful spirit children who now regularly join us. When I asked Romanov about Johnny he told me Johnny was one of the children in the hospital who had died of cancer, and that the other spirit children were friends of his from the same hospital. This reminded me that a small bit of kindness can go a long, long way, and every Christmas we set up a little tree with five bright balls in honour of these lovely spirit children who make us laugh. Quite often some sitters will say Johnny has visited them; one girl even found tiny feet marks on a wet painted floor and statues moved around. Johnny confirms in the sitting that he visited and will often describe what they have in their house or what they have been up to. He especially likes cars, and sitters say they have seen a small spirit boy sitting in the passenger seat of their car.

One day while meditating Johnny asked me to get him a drum, so often when we sit in the group he bangs on the drum. We also receive other physical manifestations and can hear spirit people having long conversations. One night a medium had her ring taken off and placed on the other hand, and another sitter had her earring pulled out by a spirit. The more I work with this type of energy the more it has opened me up to becoming a better medium, and all of my mediumship qualities have vastly improved in every way. I do unfortunately have an over-sensitive nose for various smells, but it is a good tool to use when doing spirit rescue.

My guide has shown me, while in the deep trance state, pictures of what it is like in the spirit world but it all depends what the guides want to show us and depends on the ongoing dialogue within the group. The only downside of doing this type of work and working with this energy is that it really opens you up and can make you rather sensitive.

My first séance group was with several people and was run by a good teacher. It was as though it had been set up by spirit as I had heard through the grapevine the teacher was running sessions in a small hut at the back of a church that was a five-minute walk from where I lived. Funnily enough, as soon as I got there I saw one of my cats sitting on a chair in the circle, and when I said his name everyone laughed and said they thought he was lost. I furiously told him to go home, but he always ended up beating me to the session each week as he loved the psychic energy, so I left him alone.

After about a year I felt confident and my guide suggested I set up my own group of like-minded people. With séances the sitters have to be compatible with your energy, and respectful, because any silliness will affect the energy. Most traditional physical mediums like to use a cabinet or sit on a chair in a small darkened tent. At some of the séances I have been to the medium has even been tied up to prove there is no intervention with the psychical phenomena in the room. I personally never do this but rather sit in an ordinary armchair away from the sitters so as not to be touched or disturbed. When the group closes down I am called back to the room by the main sitter running the group.

In the beginning I ran my experimental sessions at the back of my home, but I had to move it away as my husband and girls starting complaining when a few of the spirit visitors decided they wanted to stay in my home and tried to move in. After upsetting the living arrangements for my whole family

– moving things around, making noises in the middle of the night and ringing the front doorbell – my unhappy, freaked out cats and angry husband indicated that enough was enough so I had to move it all up the road to my office.

My séance group, which has now been running for years, is always different. It is a closed group and not for the public, but I did allow an ABC radio team to record it a few years ago as they were interested in the work I do. I still have a lot of the same sitters, who have been very supportive to me over the years as it is the right balance. I have, however, had my fair share of nasty people who have tried to discredit me, and as soon as they leave I cut them off the oversoul of the group so they cannot tap into the work and energy. I believe in karma as I've seen it work so many times, and when you do the right thing spirit always looks after you. I have survived with this small group for many years now and we all keep being entertained and learning new things.

This is the procedure my group follows: after we have completely blackened the room out and there is no thread of light, we sit in a circle, open up with a blessing for the group, call in our guides and ask for a prayer of protection. Once the guide has finished speaking through me I stay in a trance state, bringing energy into the room, and everyone begins to sing loudly with their fingers placed on the edge of a small round table that spins around and around when the spirit people come in. Singing loudly brings in spirit phenomena, or orbs, and spirit people touch us on our bodies, rap on items in the room and talk and move about.

We are yet to manifest tokens from the spirit world but look forward to the day when we are able to manifest gifts such as crystals, coins or jewellery; I am sure with perseverance the afterlife will have more in store for us. The type of phenomena that we have witnessed is outstanding, considering we are only a small group, but to get more we will need to continue for many years as it takes heaps of dedication to do this work and the results will not come overnight. When we have finished for the night the group calls me back into the room, and we close down with a prayer and say thanks to the spirit world and ask any spirits remaining to go back into the spirit world. Afterwards we sit and chat over the night's occurrences, discussing what went on, before saying goodnight and heading home full of energy.

In my group I have a lot of ex-musicians, like myself. Some of the spirit guests we have had are John Lennon, Frank Sinatra, George Harrison, Jimmy Hendrix, Michael Jackson, Janis Joplin, David Bowie, Prince and Michael Hutchence. As well, we have been visited by actors such as Elizabeth

Taylor, Paul Walker and Joan Rivers, who is still very funny, and Doris Day, who loved animals. After she came in nearly all the sitters' pets in spirit came in as if it was a celebration; I have never experienced so many pets from the spirit world at one time! We have also been visited by the great Houdini on several occasions in our séance and been given instructions about paying attention to the cone, watching for lights and feeling different types of energy for the spirit phenomenon. In one of these sessions the cone was lifted off the spinning table and the sitters said they saw a spirit hand. These days in my trance state I seem to be working more with relatives who have passed over and who come through my voice box and give messages of love to members of the circle.

Physical mediumship requires a lot of energy, so I have a good diet with little animal protein, drink a lot of water, especially when I am working, and train at the gym or at home on a daily basis. As a rule I usually don't drink alcohol and do not take drugs, as I need to look after myself and be alert and focused. My clean living helps me to remain clear minded and focused.

## DIRECT-VOICE MEDIUMSHIP

The incredible gift of direct-voice mediumship is quite rare; I have only known of one medium, the amazing Leslie Flint, who was able to do this. With direct-voice communication the spirits speak independently of the medium, who facilitates the phenomenon rather than producing it. The role of the medium is to make the connection between the physical and spirit worlds. Trumpets are often utilised to amplify the signal, thus direct-voice mediums are sometimes known as 'trumpet mediums'. This form of mediumship permits the medium to participate in the discourse during séances since their voice is not required by the spirit to communicate. This type of mediumship is something I am still working on even though it may take me another fifteen years to achieve it. One can only hope.

## SPIRIT RESCUE (GHOST BUSTING)

I have had hundreds of cases and written many articles on the spirit rescue of earthbound spirits, so feel quite frustrated with people who say it is not possible. Any medium who says they do not exist simply doesn't have the gift or the right spirit team for the work. We are but pioneers, and there is still so much to learn and so much we don't know about the spirit world. For unknown reasons, earthbound spirits have not crossed over after death as the majority of spirits do and are often lost and confused. They congregate in older historical places, churches, shopping centres, airports, hospitals, homes, businesses, cars, train stations and almost anywhere you have people as they need our energy to stay in our dimension. They comprise a very small minority of spirits and not everyone who suicides. Earthbound spirits often have no idea they are dead and are stuck in a time warp in the astral, which is a grey dimension. They are very different from living spirits who have crossed, gotten their assessment from the elders from this life, had their contracts reviewed, received healing and once again joined their soul groups for their next lesson on earth.

Part of my life's work as a spiritual medium is releasing earthbound spirits from their entrapment on the earth's plane. This is called spirit rescue, or more popularly as 'ghost busting'. I can do this quite successfully over the phone if the client lives interstate, or go to the home, building or land area with another energy worker or dowser to meet the client. I always start at the front of the property then gradually make my way throughout the building. Before I begin my spirit team is present, so it is very common to find the lost spirit standing at the front door. They often hide under beds or in cupboards and we have to find them. As I move along I can feel the energy in my solar plexus and generally burp as I feel as though I am going to be sick. The work is very tiring as it takes a lot of energy, and usually by the end of it I am exhausted. Not everyone has this gift or can do this work; you need to be trained to be able to hear or see the spirits needing to be rescued. I have a very good spirit team to help me do this work.

While earthbound spirits do have an intelligence they do not understand they are actually dead and subsequently will not pass over. They may be earthbound for any of the following reasons:

- a fatal accident or accidental death
- suicide (and to restate: not all suicides refuse to cross)
- fear: the spirit does not want to cross over because they may be bound to the home, have unfinished business or want to stay around a loved one or pet
- their belief system: perhaps they have done something bad and think they are going to hell
- an obsessive love or greed for the material world and earthly possessions

The first thing I tell earthbound spirits is that they do not belong here, that they are stuck, confused and need to be sent off into the light. Once I have located an earthbound spirit wandering around I bring down a light, and tell the spirit it has to leave and to open its eyes and go into the portal of light. This generally takes a few seconds, and often the client will feel goosebumps or tell me all the hair on their body is sticking up as I stand back and let my spirit team do the work. If it is a dark spirit I tell it to return to where it came from and not to come back again as it is not welcome.

Sage is a good thing to use as smoking usually gets rid of unwanted spirits; they hate the smell, and it prevents them from sucking all of your energy as it makes them weak. Close all windows and doors, make sure all fire alarms are off and place a mask over the lower part of your face. Place a huge pile of loose grandfather or white sage in a pot that has aluminium foil on the bottom. Starting from the front door, light the sage then smother it with the lid of the pot so it starts to smoke. When the pot really begins to smoke move it in circles and walk room by room, opening up cupboards and smoking out all the spaces.

Once you have done this and the area is really smoky, step outside for a while. Open all doors and windows to allow positive energy to come in and negative energy and the unwanted spirits to leave. If you still have problems, call a medium who does spirit rescue work as sometimes the unwanted spirit will simply stand outside and go back in again to hide once you have left. This technique works for toxic energy and people and clears a space instantly. It will feel new and balanced and full of energy.

## WORKING WITH THE POLICE FORCE

Not everyone who is a medium or psychic is cut out to do police work. Working with the police is not something I particularly enjoy as the work is emotionally draining, but it is a wonderful service to humankind and there is no doubt the work can be incredibly important and rewarding, if you are mentally tough enough and wish to take on the challenge. I assisted the police for a while but soon realised I wanted to do other things such as mental mediumship, which I feel far more comfortable doing. We all have our strong points and some people are far better at doing the work than I am.

Recently a friend of mine went missing overseas. Her mother was frantic and asked me to try to find her, as the police had been unable to. When I called out to the spirit world I didn't hear my friend, so I told her mother she was alive, had probably got caught up and that she would hear from her in 24 hours. This did eventuate: my friend had met somebody at a nightclub and was having a little affair in a small hotel in the town before leaving the country. I'm sorry to say that in the past other stories have not had such happy endings and the lost people have experienced fates that we would never wish to envisage. It is not uncommon in a reading to find a missing person has been a victim of murder. I have always been happy to provide all the information I can to the loved one who is suffering as there are always so many unanswered questions.

I also give any information I have to other mediums working on cases but always insist they not mention my name or get me involved, because once it became known I was doing this work I was inundated with people looking for missing relatives of friends and unsolved disappearances, some of which were probably murders. I did work for a while with a group of mediums and psychics assisting the police force. We used to meet in secret every Monday night and it was interesting

work, but there were just so many missing people and cold cases that had yet to be solved. This type of work also carries a quite weird and creepy energy, as there are often dark spirits and negative energies connected to the work. My husband asked me to stop the work as he felt the energy around me and in our home had become depressing and he had a bad feeling about it. I stopped working with the other mediums on the cases but continued to train them.

I have met some really strong and brave mediums who are cut out to do this often unrewarding and thankless work of helping the police force. You are often left feeling helpless and are stuck with too many terrible images to dismiss as a witness to the cruellest and most horrendous crimes. I found sometimes, too, that the spirits I was speaking with would not give me any information about where their body was.

To those in service, if you feel you can help in some way the following is a crime lab procedure I created that will help and protect you as you enter the darkness to bring the light of hope to families and loved ones:

- Get into a comfortable position sitting upright.
- Close your eyes and take three deep, slow breaths, in through your nose and out through your mouth, relaxing every part of your body as you do so.
- In your mind's eye, imagine a red rose ... a yellow rose ...

a cat and a dog ... a beautiful green tree with large strong roots that reaches high into the sky. The part of the brain that stores and creates pictures and memories is easy to work with as it accesses your super-conscious mind, the place inside you that has the information and records from all time.

※ Feel yourself step inside a beautiful white triangle, a place of protection and unconditional love and light. Wrap this energy around you like armour made of pure white light. You are now safe and secure and no harm will come to you. Any negative or dark energy will bounce right off, transmute and go straight into a vortex of light.

※ Feel the white light of love penetrating deep into your body and into your cells as it works its way from the transpersonal point down to the top of the crown chakra, right down to the earth star, aligning all the energies together and grounding you into Mother Earth. As you count down from 10 to one, relax even more deeply and feel all your senses on alert and awakening at the same time.

※ When you finish counting you will find yourself in your own private, safe, oval-shaped crime lab that only you have access to. You can work here in privacy and safety with your loving guides and special angels to help solve potential crimes.

🌾 The crime lab is protected by archangels and the elemental kingdom, and has four towers of light that surround the room in the north, south, east and west. In the middle of the room is a large table that is surrounded by the guides who will be working with you today. They greet you as you sit and join them at the round conference table. Take time out now to ask for any information that may help to solve the case.

🌾 When you have finished, thank the guides for their help and bring yourself slowly back into your meditation room. Don't forget to ground yourself and wrap some beautiful white light around you for protection, love and healing.

**Remote viewing and psychometry,** in which a picture of or object belonging to the missing person is felt, is another way of working with police cases:

🌾 Open your crime lab as described in the previous exercise. Once there, look at the picture of or item belonging to the victim and create a connection with them. Some mediums prefer to ask the spirit of the person to speak to them directly and then consult the picture later, so feel free to work this way if it suits you.

※ Once you have made the connection ask the spirit if they are dead or alive. Whatever the answer, tell them you are there to assist them and that they are now safe and secure.

※ Write down as much information as you can. Ask the spirit what happened and where, describing a location or signpost so they can be found. Ask how many people were involved and what they looked like; ask the spirit to give you a description. Record number plates as well as the colour of any cars.

※ Pick up the person's personal object that you have to work with. Write down as many impressions as you can and ask the spirit if they have anything to give you that will help finding them.

※ Tell them that help is on the way. Cross them over if need be by bringing down a porthole of light and telling them they are safe and asking them to go into the light if they are still earthbound. Any feelings of sadness or darkness will now be released into the light for healing and transmutation.

※ Thank your guides for their assistance.

Often spirits will give you information they would not want shared with others, so only reveal what is necessary to help them. All information from the crime lab should be treated as confidential.

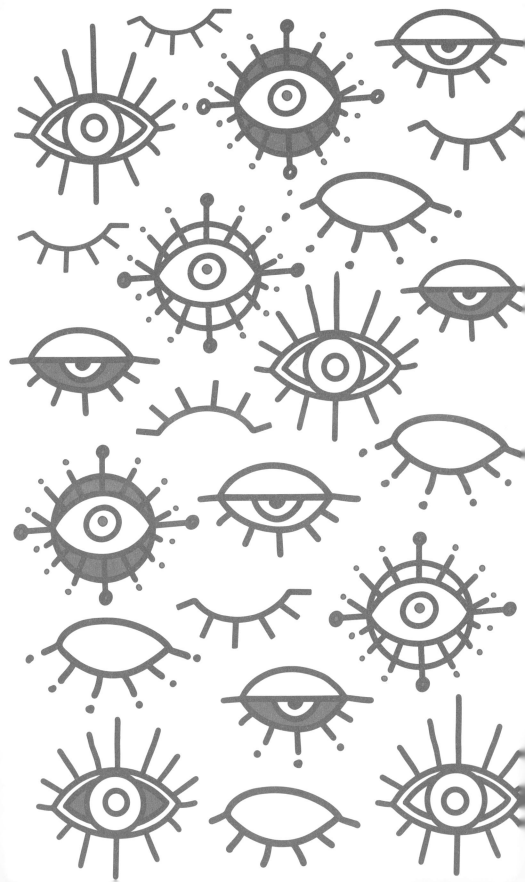

# CHAPTER 3

# Signs spirit is with us

As a working medium I have frequently been a witness to spiritual evidence that loved ones are around us, as they leave signs. In fact, anyone can experience this through dreams, smells and supernatural occurrences such as lights switching on and off, as spirit likes to play with electricity. There have been many times when I've had problems with the PA, music or lights on a stage only to find it's spirit having a field day with the electrical equipment. It takes an incredible amount of effort for spirit people to make this happen, and all just to let us know they are around and are connected to our love.

Before she died my favourite auntie always said she would leave me feathers as evidence she was around. I passed it off as a joke, although she was very glamorous, and had impeccable taste in fashion and a large collection of peacock feathers. The feathers I get from her are from the native birds in my neighbourhood, but that's fine by me as I know she's looking after me. When I first started getting piles of feathers I was convinced they were all from her and used to take them home and put them on the dining room wall, until my husband started complaining about bird lice!

My maternal grandfather was a shipwright who used to play the piano. He also collected coins, and I often find coins lying around to let me know my grandfather is around and everything is okay.

I was recently working down the coast and went to a café to have a coffee with my mum before my evening's show. Rather than a table number I was given a black ace card. Curious about what this might mean, I Googled it and saw that a lot of young people have black ace tattoos, of which I wasn't aware. That night a young man who had committed suicide wanted to get in contact with his mum and kept repeating over and over that he was sorry for making such a stupid mistake. When I called this out, a very upset woman put her arm up and said the man's name was Ace. I told the woman Ace had shown me a tattoo on his back of a black ace. The woman affirmed he had an ace tattoo on his back and that all of his friends had gotten similar tattoos in memory of him. At the end of the session I gave the woman a huge loving hug and provided further information that was for her ears only.

I have had numerous conversations with all types of spirit people from all walks of life and it always amazes me how much information they have about everything that is going on in our daily lives, sometimes down to the tiniest details. It fills me with gratitude to know this is true, as loved ones in the spirit world are always looking out for us. We live in a multidimensional world so anything is possible, and there really is no final ending at all. Some of the subtle signs or messages I have experienced are outlined below.

**Feathers:** I have seen all shapes and sizes of feathers, although these days I generally find big white ones that to me mean a miracle is about to happen: you will hear from a loved one, a healing is coming or your wishes are coming true.

**Meeting a friend you haven't seen in years:** this seems to happen out of the blue: you are thinking of a loved one and you have a chance meeting with that person. I don't believe in this is a coincidence as I believe spirit sets up these meetings.

**Coins:** every time this happens I think about my grandfather, who collected coins and marbles. Finding coins indicates a loved one's spirit is close by, and also means hearing of long awaited news.

**Dreams:** the sleep state is one of the commonest ways for a loved one to connect in spirit. It is much, much easier for communication to take place when we are relaxed and in the sleep state rather than when we are running around in our busy lives.

**Finding items that belonged to your loved ones:** out of the blue you may find something that belonged to you or a loved one that you did not know you even had. Again, it's a sign they are close by.

**A strong sense of spirit:** this happens a lot. Many clients have told me that when things are going bad or they need a bit of assistance a presence will be felt through a loved one touching them. Our loved ones are always looking out for us whether we believe it or not, and they hear us when we need them and ask for help.

**Overhearing conversations:** how many times have you overheard other people talking together about exactly what you and your loved one used to talk about all the time, such as somewhere you have wanted to go or been before?

*Music:* everyone has a special song that will remind them of a departed loved one. I've had spirit people talk about the song that was played at their funeral and about how much they loved it. Once while doing a reading for a client the people in the office next door played a song my client's husband used to play all the time. We looked at each other in awe when she realised it was his way of letting her know he was with her that day.

*Hearing a particular name:* often spirit will call out their name and you will hear someone else use the name or see it written somewhere.

*Street names:* this is uncanny to witness: you will see a street name such as 'Russell Street' or 'Stewart Road' that reminds you of a loved one in the spirit world. This is their way of letting you know they are still around and you are not forgotten.

*Numbers:* our angels and loved ones in spirit are always around us, and will remind us of this by displaying a particular number frequency such as 111, 555 or 666 that has meaning for us on a clock or the television.

**Thinking repeatedly of someone:** how many times a day do you think of a loved one in spirit? Whenever you think of them, they are thinking of you. I was recently thinking of a friend I had not seen for a while as she works in a job that does not give her the time to come to the closed séance class I have been running for years. She rang me to ask how the latest class had gone, and I told her that I had not gotten a lot of phenomena since I allowed one of the new mediums to sit next to me when I went under. His instructions were very clear: he was supposed to make contact with his own guide when he went under, observe the energy but keep giving energy to me, the table, the cone and the group energy for the experience, However, I realised he was using all my energy for himself and not contributing in any way to the group energy, thus there were no reports of flashing lights or big orbs as we had been getting previously. This was confirmed when he came out of the trance state and said he had not been paying any attention to me or the group and was just doing his own thing. When I discussed this with my friend I realised it was spirit's way of intervening and letting me know things were wrong and there was a reason for what was happening. The next day I announced on our private Facebook page that there would be no more sitters going under except me. The next session we had was a great light show and a valuable lesson to me to listen to my guides more.

**Birds:** I don't know how many times I've heard people tell me about a special bird that sits outside their window looking in. They (and me!) are convinced it is a loved one giving them a special sign they are okay and still with them in spirit.

**Spirit orbs:** these are everywhere and people quite often see them floating around, especially in photos as they are usually not visible to the naked eye. When the photo is  enlarged you will sometimes see a face that looks like somebody you know.

**Butterflies:** butterflies remind me of spirit children although this is a personal belief. Clients whose loved ones adored having butterflies in the garden see it as a special sign their loved one is letting them know they are around and have not gone far.

**Paranormal scents:** your grandmother's perfume, the aftershave your father or husband used to wear, the smoke from a pipe, the smell of the Indian food your brother loved . . . All of these scents will invoke memories of your loved ones in spirit and are an indication they are close by. An old house

I once owned was haunted by the couple who had previously lived there. Every afternoon at 5 pm we would hear the sound of a walking frame being dragged along the carpet, and my daughter would yell out: 'Mum, old Mrs Robinson's back again. She's done a smelly wee on Dad's rug.'

**Beloved pets:** clients constantly relate how often they will feel their deceased pet dog on the bed, their cat winding around their legs or the cry of the beloved horse they had to put down. My client Sally said she would often wake up from a deep sleep and feel her dog Benny in spirit sitting on her feet, which was something he had always done in the living.

**Spirit interventions:** if things are going badly you can ask your loved ones for help, and generally within 24 hours you will get a sign that all is well. Spirits hears and knows all our needs.

**Universal messages:** when you are down in the dumps you may suddenly see angel wings in the clouds or an image of Jesus or whatever god you follow, which are indications that help is on the way. Universal love is everywhere.

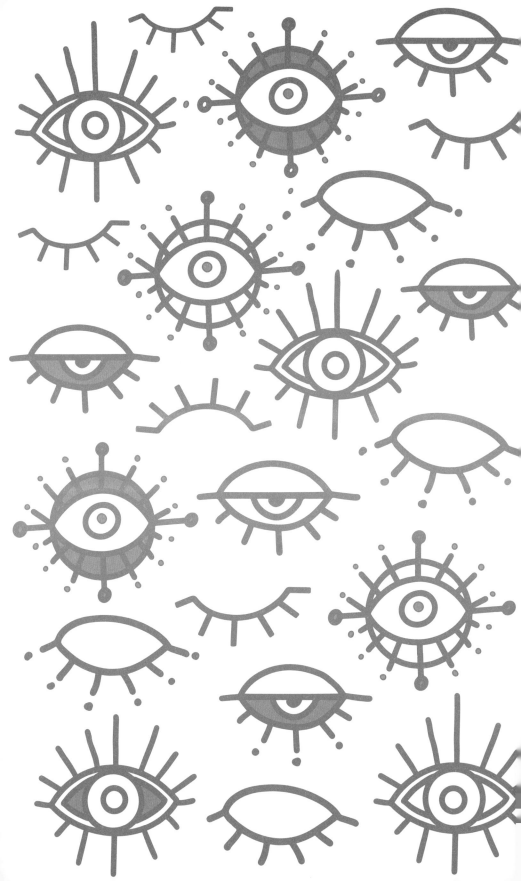

# CHAPTER 4

# Suicide: a difficult subject

To lose someone from suicide is incredibly painful, as you never understand why they took their own life and wonder if there was anything you could have done to prevent it. As a working medium I have met so many people from all walks of life who have lost a loved one in this tragic way, and have cried along with them. It is a very sensitive subject and is close to my own heart, as I have experienced the suicidal death of a loved one in my father's family.

The wonderful thing about being a medium and doing the work I do is that I can talk to people in spirit who have passed over to the other side or are earthbound, so it is easy for me to understand things a lot better than loved ones who are left behind. There can be many misunderstandings regarding suicide and the afterlife, and it is important for those left grieving to understand their loved ones are not continuing to suffer on the other side. Following are some of the commonest questions I'm asked regarding a spirit connection with someone who has taken their own life.

**If you kill yourself are you punished and sent to hell?**
You are not punished for suicide, as it is part of the contract you chose to experience when you came down to earth for that life. When you die your loving guide usually takes you straight over to the other side, where you get healing, meet loved ones already there in the spirit world and go back to your counsel and soul groups until it is your time to come back to earth as a soul for

lessons and learning. There is no such thing as hell.

When people suicide, however, it can take them a while to heal and often they are taken by their guide to a holding place where they are worked on until they are ready to move on. Sometimes the spirit world will organise a medium through a client to help them move on, and it is up to us to tell them they are dead and that they need to cross over.

**Is it harder to make contact with a spirit who has committed suicide?** I have not experienced this problem because once the spirit has crossed it is easy to communicate as the link is very clear. I've known spirits who *were* hard to communicate with as they were stuck in the astral for some reason, but they can be easily moved on by a medium or over time by their guides. Some souls may take longer or spend extra time in the healing places in the spirit world, but usually they are keen to move on so they can get a message of love across to their loved ones here on earth.

**Do people really mean to kill themselves?** I have spoken to only a handful of spirit people who have said that they planned their suicide because they could not go on. Mostly though I speak with younger people, who tell me how stupid they were, wish they had not done it and want to come back as fast as they can in another lifetime to be with their loved ones. Obviously there is no turning back and the loved ones are left bereft.

It brings tears to my eyes for these wretched souls and what they must have been going through before their time of death. The majority of suicides I have worked with had mental health issues that were not dealt with or diagnosed adequately. As a society we need to recognise the warning signs given out by our loved ones or people we know who may be struggling with themselves and their lives. There are some things you can watch for that will indicate someone who is depressed and may be at risk of suicide. These include:

- expressions of hopelessness or helplessness
- changed eating or sleeping habits
- a dramatic change in personality or appearance or irrational or bizarre behaviour, not wanting to communicate and locking themselves away
- an overwhelming sense of shame of guilt for no reason.

Even though you may notice warning signs, which may not always be present, there is no guarantee there is anything you can do to stop someone from committing suicide. However, always be ready to listen to what they have to say even if it sounds ridiculous. The most effective thing to do for people who are thinking of taking their own lives is to help change the stigma associated with mental illness and encourage a greater focus on mental health and inclusion programs throughout your local and national area. I have heard my clients say over and over that they wish they could have done something and they will often blame themselves for years afterwards, which is not what the person who suicided wanted or intended.

If you feel you or a loved one needs help dealing with suicidal help, please immediately contact any of the organisations listed here as they can provide excellent assistance and guidance:

> ❊ Lifeline Australia, 13 11 14, www.lifeline.org.au
> ❊ Beyond Blue 1300 224 636 www.beyond blue.org.au
> ❊ headspace (national youth mental health foundation), (03) 9027 0100, www.headspace.org.au
> ❊ Black Dog Institute, www.blackdoginstitute.org.au
> ❊ Kids Helpline (for young people aged from 5 to 25 years), 1800 551 800, www.kidshelpline.com.au
> ❊ Suicide Callback Service 1300 659 467, www.suicidecallbackservice.org.au
> ❊ Mensline Australia, 1300 789 978, www.mensline.org.au

# CHAPTER 5

# Gifts to work with: the clairs

We're all aware of our five senses – seeing, hearing, feeling, smelling and tasting – but you may not know there are psychic abilities that correspond with those five senses. There is also one other clair: claircognizance, or clear knowing. When a medium connects with their spirit energy their body and mind will become flooded with thoughts, feelings, images, sounds, tastes and smells. You may have a dominant clair or have abilities in a few of them if not all, but whatever skill you have the spirit will use as they make a great effort to get a message across. Below is a description of each of the clairs to help you determine which of them you are dominant in.

## CLAIRVOYANCE: CLEAR SEEING

Clairvoyance, or the ability to see anything that is not physically present such as objects, people, animals or places, brings divine guidance as still pictures or miniature movies in your mind. Often when I am doing a reading for someone it is normal to see the spirit person in my head very clearly; I can describe them and what they look like as though I'm watching a movie. I am also shown landscapes, people's faces, objects and sometimes pictures. In order to expand this I meditate daily so it becomes easier to open my mind.

## CLAIRAUDIENCE: CLEAR HEARING

Clairaudience is the ability to hear the voices or thoughts of spirits. When I work I can hear the spirit speaker as though I am on the telephone and can always tell if it's a female or a male. I will often detect accents, and if the person is a non-English speaker they will relay their messages to me in English or a language I can easily relate to my client. The grandmother of one recent client was Norwegian and the message was half in English and half in Norwegian, which delighted my client. Sometimes the connection is very clear and sometimes not, in which case I tell the spirit to speak up. If the spirit was not a big communicator while living they will generally be the same in the spirit world. Some mediums will receive only thoughts.

## CLAIRSENTIENCE: CLEAR FEELING

Clairsentience involves receiving divine guidance as emotions or physical sensations, such as smells, tightened muscles or touches. The medium will have an impression of what the spirit wants to communicate or feel sensations instilled by the spirit. The medium may also be able to take on the ailments of the spirit, feeling the same physical problems or conditions the person had before death. All these signs are proof of survival for the sitter.

## CLAIRSALIENCE: CLEAR SMELLING

Clairsalience is also known as paranormal smelling or psychic smelling. The range of smells can be wide, from the odour of flowers and perfumes to foul or putrid smells. Though often part of a wider set of unexplained smells, single scents can sometimes indicate a ghostly presence. A person with clairsalience doesn't smell normal smells but rather smells energies, which are transformed into scents in the nose; the origin of the energy that is smelt isn't always known. Often you can smell cigarette smoke, alcohol, aftershave, perfume, urine or food, things the spirit was involved with when they were among the living and the client will recognise instantly. Sometimes the spirit smell will linger for days until their message has been relayed or until they are told to leave. I have experienced this many times, and the smells can be very distinctive and strong.

## CLAIRGUSTANCE: CLEAR TASTING

Clairgustance is the ability to receive taste impressions from spirit. I've lost count of the times I've tasted cakes, baked meals or treats the spirit people loved to eat or drink when among the living; it tells me how much they miss these things. The loved one of a particular client came through talking about Coca-Cola, and after a while I could taste it in my mouth. My client said he used to always scold his wife about drinking it, which provided evidence she was sitting by his side. I also have a tendency to burp, which I can't control as I can taste or feel illness in the body of the spirit person.

## CLAIRCOGNIZANCE: CLEAR KNOWING

Claircognizance is having knowledge of people or events without knowing how you came by the knowledge; it won't be received through normal or psychic senses but will rather just pop into your head. Mediums are obviously highly intuitive and will just 'know' the facts with a sense of certainty.

## DEVELOPMENT EXERCISES FOR YOUR CLAIRS

*Clairvoyance:* sit in a comfortable position with your feet firmly on the ground. Imagine a beautiful golden light ball of energy coming up from the earth star at the bottom of your feet, right up to the transpersonal point 5 centimetres above the crown chakra or energy centre of the top of the head. Imagine a tight string of light connecting all of your energy centres. Continue breathing very slowly in and out and, as you do so, release any darkness, tightness, blockages or negativity from your body into the light, into the light, into spirit.

Feel your lungs expand with fresh, pure universal energy. Feel your third eye centre, which is in the middle of your forehead and goes right down to your nose. Imagine it being like a muscle. As you continue breathing with your eyes closed, feel your third eye slowly open and close, open and close. Feel your third eye opening more and more and energy expanding into the room. Continue to send golden light through your third eye. As you are clearing and exercising your third eye, release any negative thoughts about seeing. Know, and say: 'I am the god energy within; I am a pure and clear channel of love and light. Let love and light be my guide.'

*Chanting*, which is speaking or singing words or sounds with one or two pitches called reciting tones, will also help your third eye open as it raises your consciousness, vibration and energy. Chanting may range from simple melodies involving sounds to highly complex musical structures that are continually repeated until you feel you have had enough. It is like a prayer, and is used a lot in spiritual practices.

Sit or stand in a comfortable position and loudly chant these sounds, repeating each one separately: 'aum', 'auh' and 'om'. When you have finished chanting you will feel light-headed and good within yourself, as it will clear your mind. It will also give you insight into any situation or problem you are having in your life as it changes the thought process and dismisses any negative thoughts. For more effective results call on the archangels Michael, Raphael, Uriel and Gabriel for assistance, healing and guidance.

*Clairaudience:* learn to listen to and be aware of the stillness around you. Each day, count mentally how many sounds you can hear. Close your eyes and start by listening to sounds around your home, office or study. Take a walk in nature and listen to everything around you: the earth, trees, plants, birds and insects. You will be surprised when you take the time to listen just how many different sounds you will hear. Every living thing around you is energy, and with patience and practice you will be able to hear it.

Listen to the words and sounds of music, as spirit will often use this as a signpost they are around. Pay more attention to the sound of your family's, friends' and children's voices. Clear your ear chakras or ear energy centres with white light; they are located on the outside of your ear. Imagine you have an invisible dial inside your eye that can be dialled up when needed. Sing vowels. Release any doubts or fears you have about clearing into the light and the god force. Call on the angels and archangels for help.

*Clairsentience:* always trust your feelings, gut instincts and impressions; your first impression of someone or something will usually be correct. Sit in a comfortable position with your feet firmly on the ground and your back straight. Bring up the golden energy from the earth star under your feet and take it up to the transpersonal point, which is above your crown chakra. Continue gently breathing in and out and, as you do this, feel yourself opening up your heart chakra and your higher heart. Call the angels and your own loving guides to assist you until you feel a warm tingling inside your body. Ask your guides to come closer; you may feel a gentle hand or energy on your face, back, leg or arm. Be aware of any smells such as perfume, scents or flowers.

As part of your awareness and emotions, honour your divine guidance, feelings and intuition. When in nature always open up and be drawn to the trees and everything else around for healing and relaxation. Try to spend time in nature every day.

*Clairsalience:* developing this sense is very enjoyable and is an exercise for two people. Get your partner to sit in a chair with a blindfold, then place things such as perfumes or aftershaves, fruits or other foods, tobacco or flowers in front of them and allow them to see what smells they can identify. You can also rub substances on your hands and let your partner smell this to see if they can identify what the smell is. The more you work with this exercise, changing the objects every time, the more you will increase your awareness. Eventually, when you ask spirit to give you a sign of who is around you they will give you certain smells to describe to your client that have a strong association with their loved one.

Every day as soon as I wake up I smell the air around me and take account of the different smells that appear. For example, I will always smell what soap my husband has used when he has showered as it is usually very distinct. I also especially love to visit markets to smell all the different sensations such as spices and foods that may remind you of another country, culture or what the spirit person likes to eat when in the living. This can help you identify where the spirit person was from, for example, smelling Asian food or curries, which are often associated with India.

Another way to develop clairsalience is being aware of what homes, experiences and people smell like. When you think of someone, what do they smell like: is it good or bad?

What does the energy around them feel like? Every time I go to a new place I always have a clear definition about how it smelt, and if it is a person my sense of smell will tell me a lot about what the person is like. This is a good clair to have when working with spirit rescue as you will be able to literally smell the spirit in the room.

**Clairgustance:** this clair is often used hand in hand with clairsalience. Once you develop and expand this ability you will literally be able to taste a lot of things so that you can describe different spirits, what they used to eat and the foods they liked and often link those tastes to different countries. I once got a very strong smell and taste of honey and was able to identify a spirit man who used to work with bees. This exercise will help you identify many of the ingredients in different foods.

Blindfold yourself and get a partner to feed you a wide variety of different foods, smelling and feeling the sensation and taste in your mouth. Once you have done this spirit may, for example, give you the smell and taste of an orange, which could mean they grew orange trees in their yard or had a significant association with oranges. You can ask the spirit person you are communicating with what they like to eat and suddenly you will smell or taste a lamb dinner in your mouth.

I have spoken to many spirit people who love to describe or talk about food as it is obviously something they don't do in the spirit world.

Another way to use clairgustance is to tune in to what a loved one or family person ate for dinner; don't be surprised when you smell and taste what they ate at the time.

If you feel you have a blockage with taste try giving yourself some healing in the throat chakra with reiki or other healing practice to activate it. I like to wear a blue lapis crystal, which helps me with my smelling and tasting abilities; this may also work for you.

**Claircognizance:** this takes many forms, as follows.

*Revelations:* you will experience a profound revelation that you are one with the angels and your god and are in the right place at the right time or that something is just meant to be. There are no coincidences in life; it is all part of your destiny or spiritual contract on earth for lessons and learning.

*Aptitudes:* you may intuitively know how to do something or fix something without even knowing how you know. I could read tarot cards and knew all the meanings without ever having studied them. People would ask me how I could do this at such a young age, but it was simply a matter of listening to the voice within and going with it, as every picture told a story and made sense to the person undertaking the reading.

*Facts:* somebody may ask you something and you know everything about it without even being aware previously you had this information.

*Insights:* for some reason you know everything about a problem as a voice inside your head told you or a spirit person gave you the information.

*Inspiration:* you will find yourself writing or saying things, ideas or concepts you have no prior understanding of. I once channelled an entire children's book on something I had no

knowledge of. I have used this ability many times when doing addresses in spiritual churches and events; I just stand aside and let the spirit speak through me on subjects I had no idea of.

*Foresight:* as you are introduced to a person or situation you will know exactly the future outcome without understanding how.

*Ingenuity:* you will find an idea about a new invention that is time or life saving or otherwise vitally needed in the world.

Always remember to have faith, never be fearful and trust in the power of spirit and divine guidance. Prayer can also be helpful. Whatever you are going through, spirit is always helping you no matter what you feel. Take time to study something you love, and exercise, meditate, forgive every single person and bad situation in your life and move on. If this is difficult, get yourself a Jesus or angel bottle and write down all your problems on a piece of paper and stick it in the bottle. Clear any clutter from your life in your office, home or wardrobe.

SPECIAL NOTE: often, people newly on the spiritual path will have only one or two channels opened, while others may be completely open and not able to control their gifts. With meditation, love, dedication and patience on a daily basis and as you give love to your craft your work for yourself and spirit this will increase in effectiveness. I highly recommend employing a respected teacher, someone with a proven track record. It really does take years of experience to work as a good medium, but your

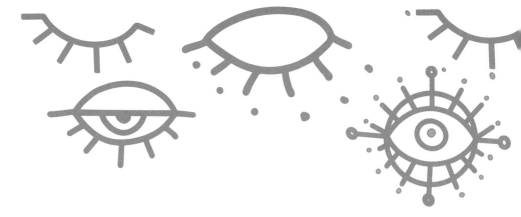

clients and audience will pull you along and give you the experience you need to do the work.

You will find your gifts will grow just as with anything you put your energy into, and spirit will help and teach you along the way. The more time and patience you put into your gifts the more you will develop and go to higher levels. If you find that you really can't improve or grow, it may be that you are meant to be a healer or psychic. I honestly believe that if something is meant to be it will happen easily, as it's all part of your spiritual contract on earth.

The world needs good mediums, psychics and healers. Know your gifts and talents, as many people will depend on you and acknowledge your good work.

# CHAPTER 6

# Spiritual churches

Spiritualist churches, in which the service is conducted by a medium, are places of worship that offer a sanctuary for spiritualism practitioners to open their awareness and experience healing. The spiritualist church was a safe and welcome haven for me when I was a young, naive woman and critical in my spiritual development as a medium. As mentioned previously, my family condemned my abilities but I couldn't just turn them off so had to hide it from them, so I needed support from another direction. It was a godsend to find a spiritual church that provided a sacred place for learning how to work with my gifts, as I had no understanding about how to control or use them and was always 'switched on', like having an electric cord straight to the spirit world. It was also was a good place to learn spiritual beliefs while working with white light, which is love and protection and is very much needed when doing the work as you are so open. The white light energy, Christ consciousness or 'source' is the highest energy you can work with.

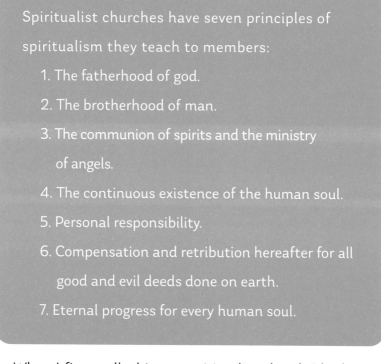

Spiritualist churches have seven principles of spiritualism they teach to members:
1. The fatherhood of god.
2. The brotherhood of man.
3. The communion of spirits and the ministry of angels.
4. The continuous existence of the human soul.
5. Personal responsibility.
6. Compensation and retribution hereafter for all good and evil deeds done on earth.
7. Eternal progress for every human soul.

When I first walked into a spiritualist church I had never seen anything like it in my life. I was used to seeing spirits or dead people hanging around and going about their business, but never so many all gathered together in one place at the same time. As I looked around me in awe, I saw great gobs of energy whirling and swishing around in the room in the air above people's heads as they sang. This really frightened me, as I had no idea what I was seeing. (I now know this was energy or spirits congregating in the hall.) As the congregation sang the energy built up and created a bridge that made it possible for the medium sitting at the front of the church to connect with loved ones on the other side. I could also smell something like old, dirty socks. Some lower types of entities often have a funny smell about them, as they have a lower vibration and dwell on the lower astral level.

Not all spirits are highly evolved, and when you go into a spiritualist church there are all types hanging around. Just because old Fred the alcoholic and drug addict has crossed over to the other side  in spirit and I or another medium can contact him does not mean he is suddenly an ascended master or someone special. Once he is dead and has safely passed over he, like everybody else before him, will have the same personality he had when he was alive. Once he is in spirit he will receive healing and will stand in front of the council with his guide and review how his life went on earth. He will have time to heal and be able to reflect on whether or not he accomplished his spiritual lessons as an immortal soul. The next time he reincarnates on earth he will have free will to choose what he wants to learn on a soul level to heal and grow and raise his own vibration.

I had finally found a place where people could help me with my abilities and, more importantly, where being psychic was quite common and accepted. I was relieved to find others who spoke my own language and who were willing to teach me everything there was to know about being a natural medium. To me, it was a lot better than a religious church because the people were kinder, like-minded, listened with patience to everything I had to say and were genuinely interested in spiritual matters. Each time I attended I heard similar stories to my own that others were going through or had experienced themselves.

The church was run by a medium and clairvoyant who was also the minister. She was a kindly woman well into her seventies with the face of an angel and a mischievous twinkle in her eye. There wasn't a mean bone in her body, and she encouraged all her students to believe in their gifts as being natural and given by god. She was a great inspiration to me as a youngster and appeared at the right time in my life because no one else I knew had any idea what I was on about. She taught me to believe in myself and my abilities and had a profound influence on me. Everybody on this planet has some type of spiritual gift, whether it is healing, channelling psychic abilities or well-honed intuition. If you want to develop these abilities it is a matter of simply believing in yourself, learning to meditate to still your mind and finding a respected teacher. I will always be grateful to my kindly minister for teaching me to trust in my inner voice and power regardless of what I was going through.

I sat with other teachers and groups over the years for development and progress, some in Australia and others from overseas; each had their own unique method and differing rates of pay depending on how well known they were. I ran my own training classes and worked with some very good mediums, which gave me a lot of satisfaction as I was able to help people grow. Some moved on and now run their own groups, teach spiritual healing or work tirelessly full time in the industry in different areas. Others work in nine-to-five jobs alongside working with their gifts and helping with the work for spirit. There are specialist colleges that train in spiritual work and also online courses; I believe when you work for service in the spirit world the doors will open to where you are meant to go. On the other hand, if you are *not* meant to work in this area the doors will close and you may be better off as a psychic or healer.

If spirit wants you to do the work then please have faith and find a group with a great teacher that fits you well. You will learn to work with your powers and gain the confidence to explore your spiritual capabilities. 'When the student is ready, the teacher will appear.' Your ability to tap into things will give you much insight into your inner world and the world around you. The more time you take to work on yourself the more it will help you to release negative patterns and karma by connecting to and working with your higher self. You will also learn to stay focused which, in turn, will help you take less time to do things. Meditation also helps you become more aware of the people around you and teaches you everything there is to know about Great Spirit (see Chapter 9). Spirit always works in so many wonderful ways and always uses us for the good of mankind in a way that we may not even know is possible.

Many developing mediums sit in circles with a highly qualified medium teacher. You may prefer to do this rather than attend a spiritual church. Trust your own intuition and only work with people you respect who are working in the light. Be very wary of those who are only into ego and power and make it their life's mission to disempower everyone else they come across by stealing their energy.

These 'energy grabbers' are so caught up in control issues and their own needs they are not aware of what they are doing and forget why they are there in the first place. I always protect myself by wrapping white light around my energy field, a most effective practice. Realise that there are wonderful true earth angels who work tirelessly for the spirit world and who would do anything for you. These people are few and far between but I never give up hope, knowing they are out there.

The beautiful aspect about this work is that your prayers to spirit will always be answered, no matter what you think or how difficult are your circumstances. It is a universal law that every action is followed by a reaction, as we are all energy. When you ask for assistance you will always receive it as spirit is always with you every single second of your life, and you are connected to spirit through your love. As previously stated, when you are ready to learn about yourself as an immortal soul the teacher will appear. With patience and dedication spirit will move you on.

## SPIRITUAL HEALING

One of the first things I learned and received during the spiritual church service was spiritual healing. It uses white light energy or universal *prana*, which comes down from your crown chakra and out through your heart and hand chakras. Spiritual healing, a simple, safe and supportive energy therapy that aims to bring balance to mind, body and soul and to stimulate the body's own natural healing ability, works with illness, dis-ease and dis-harmony in the body.  The healer links to the healing energy that is all around us then, once a connection has been made, sends the energy to the person seeking healing (who may or may not be present). Healing is complementary to traditional forms of treatment as it is non-invasive, but patients are always encouraged to seek medical advice for any conditions they have. Also, you do not have to be ill to benefit from spiritual healing as it supports good

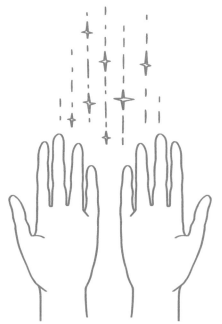

health and well-being.

In the healing part of the service a medium would place their hands on the shoulders of the person needing healing and ask for the healing energies to come in. It was remarkable to experience and it would go on for about 20 minutes. Once you opened yourself up, said a prayer and asked to work for the person's higher self you would feel the heat coming out of your hands. That sensation was a warm feeling of light or energy running throughout your whole body like a current and going into all your energy centres or chakras. After the healing was finished the energy would turn off like a tap and you would feel lightness. You could ask spirit for more healing in the next few days. Most spiritual churches continue this practice and hold sessions you can attend to receive healing for a small donation. I was once part of a Sunday healing organisation during which we would give healing to the elderly for free. Afterwards we would make them a cup of tea and have a chat; it was a wonderful time in my life.

Spiritual healer Harry Edwards was quite famous for his remarkable abilities in this area and has a healing sanctuary dedicated to his memory in England. People would say that when Harry gave absent healing they would experience a little blue light in the room that made its way to the person and to the areas that needed healing.

# CHAPTER 7

# Protection from negative energy

One of the first things I learned when I was developing as a medium was the power of protection and how to utilise it, which is mandatory in my profession as there are many different spirits and energies or different vibrations out there that are not always from the light. These spirits are mischievous and do not have our interests at heart. The can be dark (or monovalent), grey or extremely nasty, and will be very happy to take you down the wrong path while filling your head with nonsense. One essential lesson I was taught was to always ask who you are speaking with and to ask them if they come from the light. If they said 'No' or refused to answer I would tell them to go into the light, to go into the Holy Spirit in the name of Christ consciousness. Note that your own loving guides will never insist you perform a particular action; they are simply here to assist you in every aspect of your life.

I also learned to protect myself from toxic people who wanted to harm me or send me negative thought forms or energy. Unpleasant and harmful spiritual teachers can be family members, work colleagues, friends, people in high positions or partners. We can build up negative energy or negative spirits in our various environments, and although this can easily be cleared with sage we still need to protect ourselves so we can feel confident and safe. It was always a welcome relief to know that I would be safe and didn't have to worry about being psychically attacked by negative people or spirits who wished me harm.

## WORKING WITH LIGHT ENERGY

There are two types of energy – white light and dark light – that can affect us spiritually and physically. We are all made up of energy; everything around you and on the planet is made up of energy. As energy is described as being either light or dark, it is evident that colours and light itself can help you clear undesirable energies and protect you from them as well as draw in energies to your sacred and living spaces. The most universal positive light energy resonates to a white colour (actually a combination of all the colours in the spectrum) and thus harnesses the positivity from all of the colours, creating a natural balance. Using white light energy is a fundamental way to create a protective barrier to darker or imbalanced energetic forces.

Based on the power of faith and good intention, the following exercise is the first step in protecting your aura from negative energies. You can use this energy anywhere and at any time. It is especially effective if you find yourself around toxic people; just imagine the white light coming out of your finger and wrapping its beautiful energy around you or your loved ones like a protective cocoon.

**White light energy:** this form of energy is pure love from Christ consciousness. It is not only the strongest energy in the universe; it is a pure, loving, unconditional love from the highest source of all things that has powerful, protective qualities. It is beautiful, warm and nurturing to the soul. All negativity will immediately bounce off you when you work with this energy. When you need to do so all you have to do is ask with pure intention for help to be drawn into you and around you as a protective coating like an egg shell, and you will be always kept out of harm's way. At times when I feel extremely sensitive I reinforce this energy through wrapping gold around me by visualising the sun's rays as an added coat of protection and love.

Early in my training when I used white light energy I would start from my head and wrap it all around my body down to the bottoms of my feet. I would then use gold light to seal it. This worked immediately, and the more I used it the more confident I became. Every night before going to sleep I even wrapped it around my bed, which stopped nightly visitations by nosy spirits. My power was so strong with the white light energy I soon stopped using a night light next to my bed and I was never disturbed. I have taught this method to my children and will often imagine white light around people, my car, home and parents and everything I love. Your daily meditation will help you to ground yourself to these energies, and when you send love and kindness to everyone on the planet it will help raise the consciousness of all humanity. I wish one day to wrap it around the world to make it a better place.

You do not need any special tools or a specific space to perform this white light exercise; it can be performed quickly and effectively in any situation. It is most effective in a space where you feel particularly vulnerable, such as in counselling or practice rooms, your office or work space and even in your car to protect you from traffic accidents!

- Close your eyes and gently breathe in and out three times, letting all the stress from the day go.
- Imagine the white energy of pure love pouring in through the top of your head and travelling down into your body. You may begin to feel a warm sensation or a tingling on your skin.
- Direct this energy towards the space, person or object you wish to protect and imagine it surrounding them like an energetic shield.

If you feel the protected space or person is under attack again, top up their protection by repeating the exercise. Once you have surrounded yourself with white light you can activate this protective energy as a tool to protect the spaces around you. I love using this technique before going to sleep: I mentally wrap protective white light around my bed and room so that nothing can disturb my important night's sleep.

**Dark light energy:** dark energy is pure evil, fear, hatred and envy. Very easily created, it can be used to manipulate and terrify people as it plays havoc with our minds, can render us powerless and steals our energies. People who attract, use or manipulate dark energies enjoy power, come from a lower vibration and love to control others so they can make themselves feel better. Dark energy is denser, smells sweetly sick and has serious repercussions as it renders helpless all those who allow it in. People who choose to work with this energy do not work with love but come from ego. They may get what they want on a physical level, but their success over time will be a hollow victory because they will suffer emotionally in the long term and never feel fulfilled or loved in their personal relationships. They also become so obsessed with the money in their bank accounts that it can never be enough and will give them little pleasure.

## PSYCHIC ATTACK

When I first started opening up energetically and learning about energy I was often psychically attacked by menacing spirits. In the middle of the night I would feel something pressing down on me or trying to suffocate me and would wake up screaming, scaring the life out of my poor husband who would jump out of the bed thinking someone was trying to kill him. It was like a really scary nightmare except I could feel myself being strangled. When I looked around I could see there were no spirits in the room but I could certainly feel a nasty energy around me, and I would burp and feel sick in the stomach. This would leave me terrified and it would take me hours to get back to sleep; so much would be going on in my head. Whenever I had these psychic attacks the bad feelings would take ages to go away and I would kick myself for not putting white light energy around the room for protection before going to sleep.

My meditation teacher couldn't give me any answers as this had never happened to her; she suggested I work to lift my vibration as it was probably at a very low rate. I felt that what she was saying was not the solution as it did not feel right and deep down I knew that spirit was trying to teach me something. I later learned these episodes were psychic attacks, a build up of negative energy in my room. I meditated and was told by my guides that it was spirits I was attracting along with unfavourable energy from people who did not like me. I began to burn sage or sweep the room with white light, and the adverse energy would immediately disappear. I would then imagine the person who didn't like me in a pink bubble of love and ask for their forgiveness.

In a meditation class I attended for years I had an unpleasant relationship with another woman in the group that I sensed was probably a past-life connection. No matter what I said or did she did not appear to warm to me and I felt that she never would. I gave up trying to be friendly and ignored her, but every time I saw her I would go home feeling completely drained and needing to go straight to bed, even in the middle of the day. It was obvious she did not want me there and I could literally feel invisible knives in my back and pain in my solar plexus. I thought of her as a psychic vampire. White Feather told me the group was the wrong energy for me anyway, that I had learned all I could in that particular group and it was time to move on. I started to run my own groups and have never looked back.

If we have fallouts, bad connections or altercations with people or are not on the same wavelength they can send us negative energy or thought forms. We will know because you will be able to feel the adverse energy around you. To stop a potential psychic attack it is best to dispose of any gifts or things the person has given you throughout your relationship in order to break the connection. If you have trouble letting these things go, at least sage them thoroughly. This is easily done, and once you have sent the person love and released them from their contract with you the bad energy will slowly dissipate. I also sage my home as a precaution whenever negative people are around.

Another thing I do when I'm feeling really low on energy or drained is to recall my energy. When I came home from my day shift at the hospital I would feel so tired I could hardly walk, and everybody in the house, including the cats, would hide from me because they knew what a bad mood I was in. While lying on my bed I would call back all the energy that had been taken during my shift. Slowly, after a good cup of tea, I could feel my energy return and would be ready to enjoy the evening with my family.

## PROTECTING YOUR ENVIRONMENT

I am a natural empath and thus very sensitive as I am so open to all types of energy. This makes me more aware of not only protecting myself, my home, family, pets and car but also my place of work. Not everyone on the planet is love and light and I have been burnt by other light workers, or negative energy has been directed towards me by people who wish me harm. Jealousy, resentment, fear and hate engender terrible thought forms that can lead to psychic attack.

We once lived next door to a terrible man who was obviously suffering from stress; he was married to his second wife and had an expensive lifestyle. He took offence to everything we did and was constantly attacking us verbally or playing loud music that made our house rock. I set up an energy filtration system that worked really well and kept his bad energy away until we decided to move on to a quieter place. Thinking I did not have to worry any more as we had sold the property I took down the energy filter, but just before we left the neighbour attacked my husband, punching him in the head and pushing him down to the ground. I marched furiously over to his house and told him there would be retribution for what he did; he yelled at me, telling me I was a witch and that nothing would happen to him. After I called on the lords of karma I heard he had lost his job and that he was having an affair with another woman.

This simple exercise will block negativity from entering your home and space and harmonise the environment around you.

As you open yourself up with a small prayer, call on the guardians, angels and beings of light to create a protective boundary and fence of light all around your selected space to stop negative energy coming your way. Say out loud:

*'I ask the guardians of light to deflect all negativity from my environment and space and reflect love from my environment and space to defuse any negative and imbalance.'*

Place this energy all around the perimeter of the space and position a mirror on the outside to reflect any negative energy for extra protection. Now ask:

'Please make everything that is mine safe within the boundaries and deflect everything that is not away from my environment and space with love.'

This will make your space invisible. Any negative people who enter will leave their negativity at the gate or the front of the protective wall you have set up. As you look out into the world you will see that your space is not affected. You won't have problems with theft, and your space will always be safe. Make sure you perform this exercise at least once a week; it is bombproof and always works.

## PROTECTING OTHERS FROM YOUR NEGATIVITY

Often in life we can get angry and release our feelings of frustration, resentment and anger on others. As we work more on ourselves our mind power will become stronger, and it can be detrimental to those around us by creating psychic attack or negative thought forms without us understanding how powerful our mind power is. You will learn as you move along the spiritual path that you have personal responsibility and need to be more aware of the people around you. Psychic attack is very destructive and unpleasant to receive and we sometimes do it subconsciously via our adverse thoughts of resentment or jealousy. It can take a while to learn how to control our emotions as we go through the trials and tribulations of life. You may have been told to putt names in the freezer to stop negativity or psychic attack, but it is far better to forgive and send out love. This is the safest and strongest way to feel balanced and have love in your life.

## PROTECTING YOURSELF FROM NEGATIVITY

All matter, including all living things, have an energy field or 'aura'. Negativity leads us down a very bleak and sad path and takes us away from our true purpose. To heal or improve your own energy you can take a walk in nature, , swim in the sea or other body of water, immerse yourself in a salt or Epsom bath, meditate, exercise, hug a tree or dance and so on. All of these activities will clear your energy field. You can also wear bright colours to raise your energy; I wear red pants and red underwear to give me super powers!

The following can be signs you are being drained of energy:

* sudden exhaustion as if you have no energy
* a craving for sweet things; hunger or lack of hunger for no reason
* inability to concentrate and being distracted
* feeling sad, stuck and unmotivated to do the things you normally love to do
* wanting to sleep all the time
* wanting to withdraw from the world

In the worst-case scenario you will not be your happy self or will feel worthless. You want to give up on everything or want to end it all. **If this is the case please see a good therapist or doctor, as you may have serious depression.**

Below is a list of things that will help you to clear your energy field:

- Use white light energy at all times by running it all around you or create a protective egg shell.
- Use your imagination to see and feel a dark blue magical cloak wrapping all around you; this will add extra protection.
- Pull your energy in close to your body, so you become more invisible and others may not notice you.
- Close down all your chakras after meditation and working with spirit by imagining you are turning off little lights.
- Clear any negative energy or wandering spirits away by smudging your aura with grandfather sage or gum leaves.
- Burn or apply to the skin essential oils such as sandalwood, frankincense, lavender, rose and pine. Cedar is good for soothing, uplifting and replacing negativity with optimism. Cypress with lemon and geranium is beneficial for healing and cleansing. Try thyme, sage, peppermint and rosemary as cleansers to bring in love and enhance mental powers.
- Practise grounding by standing barefoot on the grass or soil. Raise your hands above your head while

breathing in and extend your fingers, slowly lowering them towards the earth while breathing in and then lowering your arms towards the ground.

- Monitor your thought forms at all times: 'What we believe we become.' Listen only to positive thought forms and be aware of negative patterns or people in your life, including your own family members. You deserve to have a good life, so forgive and walk away.
- See a good counsellor or spiritual healer for advice if you are not coping with your life.
- Open all your windows and allow fresh air in.
- Do the white room exercise (see later in this chapter).
- Cut any adverse ties (see later in this chapter).
- Always close down after a session and sweep white light through your energy centres.

## PSYCHIC THOUGHT FORMS

Many of my clients have asked me why people become jealous and are unsupportive? It can be something that was carried through from past lives or a negative energy that exists in your aura. Our thought forms deal with the conceptions and misconceptions about what we believe is real to us; a negative thought form or belief occurs when we are feel very unhappy within ourselves; it can grow and become our focus, and other people will be able to sense it. Negative energy can manifest in relationships, money issues or feelings of betrayal; it must be acknowledged and cleared.

The following exercise can be used regularly to stop you from building up negative energy. Affirmations are also good for building positive thought forms as they will change your thought processes.

- Go into your sacred space and light a candle.
- Visualise a beautiful pink bubble in front of you attached by a string to your heart.
- Feel all the negativity you have about yourself and fill the balloon with it. Ask it to leave.
- Take a deep breath in and out say: 'With my free will I now surrender all negative thought forms about myself from my aura. I call on my highest self, the angels and universal healers to help me remove this energy and disconnect me from this negative energy. I ask the negative energy to be transformed into positive energy and ask that I be healed.'
- Cut the string and release the balloon into the light, into the holy kingdom for healing and transmutation.

## WHITE ROOM EXERCISE

This is an easy and powerful technique to clear any spirit attachments, entities, psychic attack or darkness from your energy field. It only takes a couple of minutes and is useful for anyone who does healing work or is a light worker. It can be used as many times as you like, although daily is ideal.

I use this procedure often with clients, friends, children and family, as it can be used every day and works immediately on the aura or energy field. I also use it myself if things are not going well or if I feel I have attracted negative energy, ill intentions or attachment from being run down or mixing with toxic energies. The white light is a very powerful force that can protect you from anything; you will always feel safe and secure when you use this energy. There are no forces in the universe that can penetrate that energy. Believe it, and know it.

- Close your eyes and take three deep breaths in through your nose and out through your mouth. When you are feeling calm begin.
- When you feel calm, imagine you are in a white room. If you can't see it, feel it.
- Look to the left, and if you see anything standing

there such as a dark shadow, person, pretend guide or anything else command it to leave and go into the light. Keep doing this process until there is nothing there, as it is important to clear the space.

- ⚬ Look to the right and repeat the process.
- ⚬ Look to the front, and if you see anything there ask it to leave.
- ⚬ Look to the back. If it is clear you can wrap a white light of protective love around you, followed by a beautiful blue light and finally a gold light.
- ⚬ Open your eyes. You should feel lighter.
- ⚬ Close down your chakras when the session is completed and sweep white light through your energy centres.

## CUTTING TIES EXERCISE

This exercise is good for cutting off old and worn energy that no longer serves you from people that are no longer in your life or mean you harm; it helps both parties move on. It can also get rid of negative energy you may have been carrying towards that person or other people who have been tuning in to any old destructive patterning you have been carrying. I have tried this many times and always get immediate results:

- Visualise a blue figure eight that has gold in the middle of the circles. Put yourself in one circle and the person whose energy you want to cut ties with in the other.
- Imagine old ropes or vines wrapping around you.
- Take note of what colour the energy within the ropes is, whether it is thick or thin and how it makes you feel.
- Mentally cut the ropes off with a sword, knife or pair of scissors. When you have done this, cut the centre of the figure eight and blow the person away into a big pink bubble of love. This is your healing bubble or healing room in which no harm can come to anyone as it is a sacred place of love.
- In your mind, tell the person what you think of them. Tell them who you are as a person and how you want to be treated in all your personal relationships. Tell them you love them and forgive them and that the contract you once had is now terminated.
- Bless the person, say goodbye and step out of the healing bubble. Send it full of green healing light into the source of love.
- Close down all your chakras and sweep white light through your energy centres.

# CHAPTER 8

# Boundaries

Setting up boundaries early in life is an integral part of our development as a soul. Boundaries form the foundation of our lives, provide a road map to a relatively stress-free existence and are a tool for enjoying healthy relationships. Boundaries are simple guidelines, rules or limits you create to identify reasonable, safe and permissible ways for other people to behave towards you. When someone such as a work colleague, boss, friend, family member, partner or neighbour behaves in a way that makes you feel uncomfortable, compromised or stressed or passes certain limits it is up to you to respond in the correct way.

Boundaries comprise a life skill that is built from your belief system, opinions, attitudes, past experiences and social learning. They teach you to have a voice and to set distances from overbearing and insensitive people who are happy to invade your space, press your buttons for their own benefit and make you feel spiritually, emotionally, mentally and psychologically overwhelmed, unprotected and drained. Never be afraid to say 'No' to any situation you find yourself in that makes you feel compromised, and have the courage to walk away from toxic people and offensive behaviour that does not have your best interests at heart. Here are the best ways to learn about boundaries.

*Always trust your feelings and honour what you know to be real,* as tuning in to your feelings and emotions is the key to open the doorway to your own sacred, inner wisdom. Fear, feeling unappreciated or anxious, resentment, disappointment and anger are just a few emotions we often experience when we are compromised or feel unprotected in any given situation. Ask yourself: 'Why am I feeling these emotions?'

*Learn your own limits what feels right and what does not.* Always honour your own feelings or gut instincts or how you feel in your body, as these feelings are always true. Guilt often comes when someone imposes their own expectations, views or values onto us.

*Have the confidence to speak up and be heard.* Often we make the mistake of being silent or tense and not having the courage to speak up, but if the bad behaviour continues it is usually best to be direct. Learn to respectfully give an opinion about what you feel is important to you, as we are all different. For example: 'I don't give you permission to speak to me in this way.' The person may not like it, but once stated gently they will be aware they are out of line and hopefully amend their behaviour.

*Never allow people to make you feel guilty or think you owe them something.* It is better to speak your piece than feel guilty, drained or taken advantage of. Remember: healthy boundaries are a sign of self-respect and self-love.

*If you are having problems with boundaries that are important to you, join a group of like-minded people who you can share your interests with.* You could also seek counselling or other ways of supporting yourself and your well-being.

*Keep a diary of how far you have come.* When you read back over what you have written you will see how your life has changed and how confident you have become. Creating and keeping boundaries is an art, but it is very easy to learn. Once you learn to say 'No' the rest is easy.

*Meditate or join a spiritual group of like-minded people.* When you take the time to go within you will be able to tap into your own higher self, soul and intuition. The soul has the memories of every lifetime you have ever lived and has the answers to any problems in life. Through meditation you will learn about the afterlife and the guides, spiritual helpers and angels who come with that reality and are always here to help you.

# CHAPTER 9

# Meditation

Meditation is a very important tool to help you open your awareness on your spiritual journey. Not only does it help you to focus so you can pull in your energies, it also helps you to become much more calm, relaxed and focused. Twenty minutes of meditation is equal to four hours' sleep, as we are working on the theta level. I meditate or pray every day for guidance. Meditation can also move you to a higher vibration level or frequency, connecting to your higher self, your angel and your own loving spiritual guides. Life will become more rewarding as you get better at going with the flow and not get caught up in all of the small stuff. When you learn to go within you will connect daily with the divine source of all things.

For effective meditation, create a small space in your home you can call your own, in which you feel safe and secure and where no one can interrupt you. It will be best if you can meditate at the same time/s each day, as by doing this you are making a date with your guide. Once a day would be good, but twice a day would be even better. Having said this, please be aware that there really are no rules and you should carry out the meditation in whatever way works for you.

## CREATING AN ALTAR OR SACRED SPACE FOR MEDITATION

For your altar, decorate a small table or bench with fresh flowers, pictures, statues, crystals, rocks, shells, feathers, icons, an incense burner, candles or whatever you fancy. Ask your angels to join you as you create this special and beautiful work of art. Incense or essential oils for a special aroma while you are meditating would also be nice. Harp and flute music or bells will attract loving angels into your sacred space, but any relaxing music will do.

Nature is an ideal place to connect through meditation with the divine source, whether it is the bush, beach or just a beautiful garden full of flowers and trees. In those places you  can get help from the elemental kingdom, which is full of tiny nature spirits that have been with us since the beginning of time. The undines are beautiful water fairies, graceful little winged creatures that live around rocky pools. The air spirits known as sylphs are tiny spirits full of ideas and inspiration. Salamanders are fire spirits, and the earth spirits are known as gnomes, goblins, elves and pixies. If you are unable to utilise your own sacred space you can simply surround yourself with light and take five or 10 minutes to relax and raise your consciousness and connect with the divine source with intention. A small prayer may also help.

As you begin to meditate on a daily basis you will realise what an important tool meditation really is. Not only will you look a lot better and have more energy, you will also begin to wonder exactly how you ever coped without it. You will have more clarity and perception and be able to focus more effectively with everything in your life. Many successful people meditate and are thus able to focus on their desired outcomes. By going within you will be able to manifest and create your own reality.

## MEDITATION FOR YOUR HIGHER SELF

Once you begin meditating and going within you will also begin to recognise various levels of consciousness. In mediumship we learn who the main guide, guardian or gatekeeper is that looks after our soul. As we move on, we come to know how loving and kind our gatekeeper is and how to develop a strong, protective and deeply trusting bond with them. We ourselves have a higher self, or what I call the soul energy, that lives on through all eternity and is here for lessons and learning on earth. I discovered this aspect of myself when I worked with the Michael Newton Institute for Life Between Lives Hypnotherapy, and was told during deep hypnosis and while in the spirit world that *Saku* was my spiritual name or higher self. Saku is a loving being, which is why I have always known it is my spiritual purpose to help people. I have been driven to work in service, in no matter what field, and my life has certainly been colourful! It explains why I wanted to be a nurse earlier in life and why I have studied so many healing modalities. I also have a strong connection with and great love of nature and animals.

When you connect to your higher self, do not be afraid of letting go of attachments to the ego. Surrendering is not about losing self-empowerment; it is about gaining self-empowerment and it involves trust. When you remove the needs of the ego and allow your true destiny to materialise through the will of the soul to guide you through your life, life itself will become a rewarding journey.

Talking to the higher self meditation is a very powerful technique that can be used at all times, as long as it is used only for the highest good of yourself and another person. Often in life we experience misunderstandings and difficulties in communicating with particular people, and it can be almost impossible to talk to that person face to face. If you find this happening to you, talk to their higher selves to get your message across. Keep trying with this simple meditation until you have a positive answer from the person. Do it with only one person at a time, and know that with good intention when working with spirit miracles can happen every day. You can use this exercise with a loved one, friend, family member, lover, partner or work colleague. It will bring peace, healing, love and balance back into your life no matter how difficult the situation:

- Sit up nice and straight in a comfortable position, making sure all your chakras are in alignment.

- Take three slow, deep breaths in and out. As you do so, relax and feel any tensions in your body being released.

- Let go of all negative self-talk in your mind. If you have difficulty with this you can use the mantra 'so hum', repeating this several times as you breathe in and out.

- Visualise a pink bubble right in front of you, and if you can't see it then feel it. Place yourself inside the bubble and invite the person you want to speak with in as well.

- Tell the person what you want to say. Tell them you are sorry for any pain or disagreement you may have caused, or vice versa.

- Listen. If they do not reply, repeat again and listen carefully to what they have to say.

- Tell them gently and kindly what you need to say and tell them you forgive them and ask for their forgiveness. Ask that there be no negativity between you.

- Step out of the pink bubble and see it fill with a beautiful green light and fade far, far away, surrendering it to god and the wonderful angels to deal with.

- Close down your chakras and sweep white light through your energy centres.

## MEDITATION TO CLEAR YOUR ENERGY

The following exercise will help clear your energy, clear blocks from your chakras and ground you in the present:

- Find a quiet place or go to your sacred space and light a candle.
- Sit up nice and straight and slowly and deeply breathe in and out three times to release any blocked energy.

- Gently visualise yourself starting to bring healing energy up from the earth star into your base chakra.
- Feel it moving around your body.
- Blow any negative energy out through your mouth with your breath.
- Continue this process, moving slowly upwards and breathing in and out, releasing as you move up through all of your chakras: beginning with the base (red), sacral (orange), solar plexus (yellow), heart (green), throat (blue), third eye (indigo), crown (purple) and transpersonal point (white). Feel all of your chakras in gentle alignment.
- Expand your energy 10 centimetres from your body, then take your energy field out to the size of the room, out to the world, out to the universe and outer dimensions.
- Know you are one with everything in the universe and ask for all your soul energy that has been taken from you to come back.
- Pull your energy back close to your body and feel awareness in your heart.
- Gently wrap yourself in a beautiful cocoon of white light, then purple light, and finally with a sheaf of golden energy that washes all over you.

When you are ready to come back, feel all the energy in

your heart chakra and open your eyes. You will feel very clear, grounded and ready for a new day.

## GROUP OVERSOUL

When working with students we learn to blend our energies together so we become a collective of souls working to learn and become keen students of spirit to help ourselves and mankind. When a student joins the group they open a line of communication with their higher selves and work in alignment with love and light. Often students who are not able to attend the group due to illness or being away will still receive the healing of the night or be able to tune in to the energy from the group for help in their lives. When somebody leaves the group or no longer wishes to work with the energy it is my duty as the teacher to energetically cut all ties from the group so they are no longer able to tune in or be part of the collective oversoul of the group. I do this because in the past students kept telling me they could still feel the person in the room even though they were no longer there, that they were probably still connected to the group and 'borrowing' the energy. As well, if the student is not the right energy for the group then spirit will intervene and let them go, so often it is not because of you but the alignment of energies you are working with.

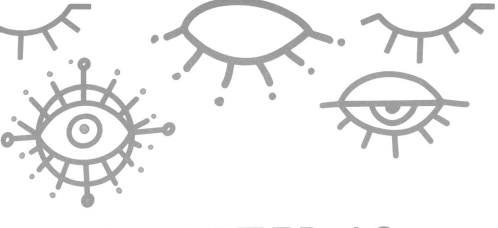

# CHAPTER 10

# The chakra system

The nine chakras are the energy centres in your body through which energy flows; they ground and protect you. Blocked energy in your centres can often lead to illness or dis-ease and can be projected onto your clients, so it is important to understand what each chakra represents and what you can do to keep this energy flowing. The final four chakras (throat, third eye, crown and transpersonal point) are critical as they assist us to achieve higher levels in our development.

### EARTH CHAKRA

**(light brown):**

this chakra stabilises you and keeps you grounded on the earth. You are able to manifest your desires and wants here.

**BASE OR ROOT CHAKRA (red, tailbone):** this foundational chakra represents survival issues such as financial independence, money and food. It influences development between the ages of 0 and 6. People with blockages in this chakra may have problems with their legs.

**SACRAL CHAKRA (orange, around the navel):** this is our connection with and ability to accept others and new experiences. It influences development between the ages of 7 and 14 and is concerned with past lives, sexuality, abundance, money issues, pleasure and sometimes mother issues.

**SOLAR PLEXUS (yellow, upper abdomen):** this chakra represents your ability to be confident and in control of your life. It influences development between the ages of 14 and 21 and is concerned with self-worth, self-confidence and control over your life.

HEART CHAKRA
**(green, chest centre):**
this chakra represents your ability to love yourself, family, friends and the people around you with inner peace and joy. It influences development between the ages of 22 and 28. A disconnection with this chakra can lead to heart attacks or other heart problems, unhappiness and a sense of being unable to connect with and manifest in the world.

THROAT CHAKRA
**(blue, throat):**
this chakra represents your ability to communicate in the world. It influences development between the ages of 29 and 35 and is concerned with self-expression, truth and channelling. A disconnection with this chakra can indicate illness or disease in the throat.

THIRD EYE CHAKRA
**(indigo, between the eyes):**
this chakra represents your ability to focus on and see the bigger picture. It influences development between the ages of 36 and 42 and is concerned with intuition, imagination, wisdom and the ability to think and make decisions. The indigo colour can be seen very clearly surrounding people who are psychic.

THE CROWN CHAKRA
**(purple, top of the head):**
this is one of the higher chakras and represents your ability to be fully connected spiritually. It influences development between the ages of 43 and 49 and is concerned with inner and outer beauty and your connection to spirit and bliss.

THE TRANSPERSONAL POINT
**(opaque):**
this chakra connects all the chakras together like a bow so

they are in alignment. From here we are able to connect to our soul groups and other dimensions.

## VISUALISING THROUGH THE CHAKRAS

With its beneficial applications, visualisation is such an extremely important tool to have; it can pave the way for creating your own alchemy or magic in life. We don't all possess exactly the same capacity for visualisation, as some are better at it than others. With a bit of practice and effort you can become extremely competent in this fine art, which will make your life a lot easier. It also helps to create the world you want to live in by imagining it in your mind then taking it even further so it becomes part of your reality.

As you understand what the chakras' colours mean you may begin to see them around people in their auras. For example, if you see yellow around someone they may be undertaking some type of study. Using your incredible imagination and with practice you will begin to see, smell and feel each colour. Learn to have fun with the colours, imagining making different shapes swirling and twirling on the canvas of your mind. Try to send them to different parts of your body.

Sit in a comfortable position and take three deep breaths in and out. Concentrate all of your attention on your breath as you slowly relax every part of your body, beginning with your head then moving slowly down to your neck, shoulders, arms, waist and so on. You will see after images on the back of your eyelids, but this will pass after a while. Just continue breathing and relaxing, letting go of all fears, worries or any insecurities; nothing bothers you. Fill your mind with colour.

**Red** governs the first chakra, the base chakra situated at the bottom of your spine. The related organs are the kidneys and the bladder, the vertebral column, the hips and legs and the adrenal gland. A healthy base chakra will keep you grounded, focused and stable so you can enjoy earth's pleasures. It can also be associated metaphysically with father issues.

**Orange** governs the second chakra, the sacral chakra situated in the lower abdomen. The related organs are the uterus, large bowel and glands of the ovaries and testes. This is about manifesting joy in the world as it is the colour of success and self-respect. It helps you express yourself with your own dreams, interests and activities. It can also be associated metaphysically with past-life issues and traumas, relationships and mother issues.

**Yellow** governs the third chakra, the solar plexus situated below the ribs. The related organs are the liver, spleen, stomach and small intestine and the gland of the pancreas.

Yellow relates to self-worth, how you feel about yourself and how the world sees you. This energy connects you to your mental self, intellect and awareness

*Green* governs the fourth chakra, the heart chakra. It brings in love, balance and harmony and is related to the heart, breasts and thymus gland. The colour is important as it is connected with self-love bringing harmony to every aspect of your life. Without it your life will become dark and sad and you may lose your way. This colour stands for everything good in life and brings in beautiful experiences and sunshine.

*Blue* governs the fifth chakra, the throat chakra, and brings in knowledge, health and communication. The related gland is the thyroid. The colour relates to self-expression, enabling you to be a creative channel of energy. This energy also connects you to wisdom and clarity.

*Indigo* governs the sixth chakra, the third eye chakra which extends from your forehead to your nose. The related gland is the pineal gland. The colour is connected with self-responsibility and following your soul path and trusting your own innate intuition. It also works with your creativity, enhancing creative talent. The term 'indigo children' or an 'indigo person' means those who are very psychic and were born extremely creative, usually in music, writing, dance and the arts.

**Violet** governs the seventh chakra, the crown chakra, which is situated at the top of the head. The colour helps you to be in union with your higher self, your soul's energy. It connects you with the higher realms and brings in wisdom and information from the spirit world. It is also about artistic talent and creativity.

## EMPOWERING WITH THE MIDDLE PILLAR

If done on a daily level this powerful exercise will clear your chakras and help purify your emotional body and energy system:

- Take time out from the world in your sacred space, sit comfortably and light a candle.
- Breathe in and out three times or until you feel completely relaxed.
- Be aware of your body, making sure your spine is straight and your chakras are all in alignment, and relax every single part of your body by tightening and letting go, releasing any stress or negative thoughts. Just let it go.
- Allow your consciousness to expand to the size of the room, the city or town around you. Take your energy out into the universe and outer dimensions.

※ Call your energy back and ask the powers of spirit for assistance.

※ Centre yourself in your power, visualising a white light going down through the transpersonal point into the crown, lightening up your head. Breathe the light down to the third eye, then the throat.

※ Continue breathing in and out and take the energy down to the heart, the back of the heart and slowly down to the solar plexus, then the sacral chakra. Feel the energy in all of these chakras.

※ Take the energy down to the base chakra and through the feet, grounding it to the earth star in the ground beneath you.

※ When you sense the light in the earth star, inhale down the vibrant power of all the brilliant spheres, lighting up your whole body through your spine and connecting deeply into the earth.

※ Bring up from the earth star a shooting fountain of light that rises above your head, showers down in two columns of brilliance on either side of your body then passes under your feet to power upwards again in a continually renewing cycle.

※ Keep repeating for 10 breaths, or until you feel you have had enough.

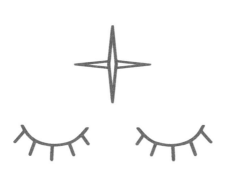

* Open your eyes and place white light all around you like a protective bubble.

## CLOSING DOWN YOUR CHAKRAS

After any type of medium work or meditation it is mandatory to close down your chakras. It is never a good thing to be open to any energies in the world as it can lead to attachments and being ungrounded. To close down your chakras:

* Sit in quiet place or your own sacred space where you will not be disturbed.
* Light a candle and perhaps some lovely incense, and have quiet, relaxing music playing in the background if you would like it.
* Imagine yourself opening up or switching on all of your energy centres like little lights.
* Imagine bringing the white light down as unconditional love through your crown chakra. Let the light expand all around you, outside and inside your body. Expand

this energy out to the room, outside to the city, even further to the country, out to the universe and outer dimensions. Imagine you are one with everything around you.

✻ Bring your energy back into the room and call back any energy that has been taken from you by others during the day or while out in the world.

✻ When you are finished, thank spirit for working with you and gently imagine all your energy centres or chakras closing down, like lights going out.

✻ Visualise the white light of protection wrapping around your whole body and once again feel yourself being anchored to the ground, or what we call the earth star.

✻ Again place with intention a beautiful white light all around your body and a golden light as an extra shield.

✻ Open your chakras by breathing slowly and imagining you are opening up to the beautiful healing energy of spirit.

✻ Sweep white light through your energy centres.

# CHAPTER 11

# Psychic links

Over the years I have run classes with great success for mediums, healers and psychics and for my own students who wish to learn how to work with their psychic and spiritual abilities. I was born a natural medium and have been able to hear and see spirit people talking from an early age. This is a gift I have but I have had to work very hard on it for many years, sitting in development circles and working on my own issues so I can not only be a better person but also surrender myself to spirit for the best service I can give. It is like an instrument you have to fine tune all the time, and you have to look after yourself so your abilities work accurately.

I chose to keep on developing my psychic abilities as they have been very helpful in my life and given me great insight. My tarot cards, coffee cup reads, crystal ball and psychometrics are all tools that help me focus inwards with my third eye and assist with futuristic reads. You don't have to utilise just a single gift but can rather use many different links with spirit to develop any number of abilities.

## LINKING IN THE CLASSROOM

Ask the students of the class to send you energy and healing to help with the reading. Say a little prayer to open yourself up to the spirit world if that works for you:

*'I am the Christ consciousness within. I am a clear and perfect conduit of love and light. Let love and light be my guide.'*

As you say the prayer feel your aura expanding and open yourself up. Ask your highest guide to stand next to you and assist you. While standing at the front of the class:

- Ask the spirit as you feel them come in if they are male or female.
- Ask any particular person you are drawn to in the class their name so you get a link to their spirit through their voice.
- Ask for validation from the student throughout the

reading, and also ask the spirit to provide proof of their existence such as their age, what they looked like, how they died, where they lived, how many children they had, their habits or any pets, what food they liked and so on. Get as much information as you can. Sometimes the link may be weak; if it is, ask the spirit to come closer or speak louder, or to show you what they want to say.

☀ Ask the spirit for the message they wish to convey. Once the link has broken tell the student and close down and move on to somebody else, as often spirit will work fast.

Always close down after a session and sweep white light through your energy centres.

## LINKING THROUGH YOUR AURA

For this exercise it is good to start off in pairs:

☀ Prepare yourself psychically by opening all your energy centres or chakras and bringing white light in to wrap around yourself. This is your protection.

☀ Sit opposite your partner and focus your attention on your solar plexus.

❄ Feel your own aura expand so that it embraces the aura of the other person.

❄ Give a reading for that person, detailing anything you pick up.

❄ Have a short break then go to the next phase.

❄ Without looking at your partner, focus all your attention on your throat and brow centres. Ask your guide or guides to bring in someone from the spirit realm whom your partner knows (from your family or someone they have known in this life or can relate to).

❄ Ask the spirit to come closer into your energy as if they were standing in your own shoes and occupying the same mental space.

❄ Concentrate on them as if you are becoming the same person. If this is too much for you, ask them to step back slightly. Let all the emotions, words and images flow through as if they were your own. Do not say anything until you have a link; concentrate only on the spirit who has come in.

❄ Ask the spirit validation questions as in the previous exercise.

Close down all your chakras by sweeping white light through your aura.

## LINKING THROUGH NUMBERS

I began using psychic links via numbers when I started working in television and radio, as sometimes it takes time to bring a spirit person in and this is a way to get a fast link. There is nothing worse if you are in the entertainment industry than struggling to get a link, as this will open you up to ridicule and make you look unprofessional. Linking through numbers is a psychic link that, once established, will allow a medium to reach a higher level of connection with a loved one.

A very quick psychic link can be made by adding up the numbers in a person's birth date; for example, a birth date of 18/3/1957 gives us the number 7:

$$1 + 8 + 3 + 1 + 9 + 5 + 7 = 34$$

$$3 + 4 = 7$$

If you have made a link but none of the information you receive is resonating with your client, stop and start again as you have it wrong. Don't make the mistake of insisting you have it right and the client has it wrong. If you have two grandfather (or similar) spirits around you giving conflicting information, ask one of them to move away and the other one to step forward and give the second reading later. Ask your guide to step in and help you with this.

Below is an indication of what the numbers from 1 to 9 may be referencing.

**1:** new beginnings, patience, leaving the past behind, stepping out into the unknown.

**2:** patience is the key word here, as things won't happen fast and need to be undertaken slowly. It can also mean relationships, and that it is a good year for romance.

**3:** this is expansion time, fun, believing in yourself, socialising, getting out there. This year will be very different from the prior year.

**4:** getting your life in order, focusing more, lots of energy, more opportunities coming as you get back to what matters to you.

**5:** freedom and change; experiencing life in a fresh place; creating new things. It can indicate an emotional year.

**6:** responsibility time; a good year for marriage and a peaceful year.

**7:** this is all about faith, as it can be a testing year where many spiritual lessons will materialise. This number is about moving forward with confidence, reviewing your life and not forcing things.

**8:** this is a year of achievement and success, of doing great things in the world. It indicates moving forward with integrity and honesty.

**9:** this is a year for endings, a good time to move on but not for new relationships as nothing will take off until next year. It is an optimum time to get rid of things that no longer serve you, such as jobs, friends, situations, problems, clutter and toxic situations. Once you clear the slate you will accomplish great things.

## DOUBLE LINKS

A double link occurs when two mediums blend their energies in harmony and work together with their individual spirit teams. Both spirit teams will provide information that can be validated by the client. Mediums must ask their guides for permission to do this and, once permission has been granted, the first medium can begin. When a link to spirit has been made by the first medium the second medium will then tune in to the energy. Gradually and with the blending of the energy they will receive a great deal of information that provides a clear picture of the spirit with whom they are communicating, each having turns and working together in perfect unison.

Always close down after a session and sweep white light through your energy centres.

## FLOWER READINGS

A flower reading is a form of earth magic from ancient times and used by healer priests and shamans as a tool to predict the future, rather like reading tea leaves or coffee cups or using tarot cards. Flowers have been communicating messages for a

long time, and there is historical evidence of folklore using flowers for inner communication and divination. It was also applied by Celtic tribes that used all sorts of plants and flowers in prediction rituals and customs Travelling Romany gypsies still sell posies of wild flowers and herbs and use flowers for fortune telling.

Flowers have a potent life force that is very healing visually, physically and emotionally. Flowers are an excellent tool for readings as they provide a good conduit for energy, optimising our psychic and mediumship abilities. They are also wonderful for new mediums as messengers of spirit. I first started reading flowers in the spiritual church and saw many other mediums work in this way. It was very helpful in the beginning, but as I advanced I found I could no longer work with flowers as I could see the spirit standing behind the client and could hear their voice in my ear.

This is how a flower reading session usually progresses:

- ❧ Everyone brings a flower from home and places it in a brown paper bag, then before the meeting starts they place their paper bag in a basket in the room. Nobody else should see what your flower looks like.
- ❧ Everyone chooses a bag as the teacher passes the basket around the room. One at a time, each person takes their flower out and opens up all of their senses – smell, taste, feelings, hearing and touch – and gives an impression of what they can sense on the flower about the person who provided it.
- ❧ Once a connection is made the flower is put down. Any spirits present are asked if they want to get a message of love across.

- ⚡ Once all the messages have been imparted, the session finishes.
- ⚡ Everyone closes down their chakras and sweeps white light through their energy centres.

## JEWELLERY READINGS

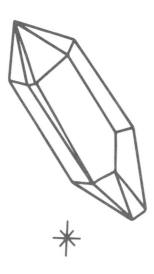

Readings with pieces of jewellery or photographs are known as 'psychometry', or token object reading. Psychometry is a great skill for beginners to practise because it really is quite easy to do. Even if it is a little tricky to pick up at first, the more you practise your psychometric skills the easier and quicker it will be for you. Always remember to have fun, and relax and don't stress yourself out over it.

When working with pieces of jewellery we receive information via an energetic psychic imprint from the person to whom the jewellery belonged or belongs. Everyone has a life force that will leave a vibration on their belongings. Jewellery reading is very similar to scrying, which is a psychic way of seeing or reading something that isn't typically visible. I have always used jewellery when wanting to receive information about a person as the metal content gives it a large amount of energy compared with pieces of clothes.

When I do a jewellery reading I always wash my hands, place a protective energy around me and open myself up, asking for guidance with my own ritual or prayer. I keep my eyes open until I start to get images in my mind and there is a movie playing there. I open up all of my senses, physical and psychic. Some of the questions I may ask are what the person is like and whether or not they are alive. If they have passed I will generally get a picture of this. I ask the spirit to come in if they are passed then, once I sense they are in the room, I place the object next to me as it is only acting as a link.

If I don't hear a voice I know they are still alive, so it is good when looking for missing people. I ask the spirit to show me a picture of where they are and usually get a picture of this in my mind or am given the name of a place. Once I have finished I will send the spirit off to the spirit world with love and blessings. I always close down after a session and sweep white light through my energy centres.

# PHOTOGRAPH READINGS

Often in mediumship readings I use a photograph of the person to read as a psychic link. I generally get a lot of impressions and then a direct communication. I used to do this so much I even found I could tap into pictures of famous people in art galleries! It is also used quite successfully for stage work. The medium will be given a photograph and will link with a person in the audience, who generally stands. Once the link is made the spirit will stand by the medium and provide information that the medium relays.

Photograph readings can be used to detect illness. If you scan the middle of your palm over the photo you will receive hot and cold impressions, which may indicate there is an area that needs attention.

For a photograph reading, once you have opened up relax and feel the back of the photo. Turn the photo around and tune your energies into it. Look at the face and connect yourself mind to mind with the person. If you cannot see clearly, use a magnifying glass and make sure you have good light. Eventually the photo will give you a psychic link and you will receive clear impressions, information and messages from the person. As you concentrate further, you will eventually begin to sense the spirit in the room and begin communication. The person in the group who is related to the deceased person in the photo will be able to clarify if the information is right or wrong. Close yourself down after all information has been imparted and sweep white light through your energy centres.

I have used this technique with deceased pets and have had many long dialogues with them. Often when a pet comes through other spirit people related to the client or student will also come into the room.

## PENDULUMS

Many people enjoy using pendulums to communicate with a spirit, find lost things or the locations of missing people and clearing chakras. You can use any type of crystal you are drawn to; I always liked to use clear quartz. The first step is to discover how you and your higher self like to communicate with your pendulum. Once you get the answer the process of using a pendulum can begin. Begin by asking questions you already know the answer to. When you have confidence you can go further and ask things you want to know. Please understand this is an effective tool for readings that should not be misused or used repeatedly to ask trivial questions such as whether or not someone loves you.

When working with a pendulum, find a quiet place for meditation where you will not be disturbed. Open up all of your senses, and ask your guides to help you work for the highest good. Place the pendulum in front of you and sweep it with white light to clear it. This has to be done each time you use it. Ask it a question that requires a 'Yes' or 'No' answer, and write the answers down on a piece of paper. For missing people, place the pendulum over a map. When it spins you have their location. When you feel the energy build up, ask the spirit to come into the room and begin the communication. After the session, send them back to the spirit world. When you have finished, close down all of your chakras and sweep white light through your energy centres.

## OUIJA BOARDS

I have to be honest and say I have never been attracted to using this type of psychic link, as I feel it can be dangerous in the wrong hands such as children or the untrained. It is not to be seen as a game as you can be opening up doorways to another dimension and negative energy you have absolutely no understanding of. Experienced mediums do use Ouija boards to get information for their sitters as it can be very effective and works quite fast. Before a session, I always set up

strong protection for myself and other sitters by saying a prayer. I also prefer to sit in dim light with candles and am very specific about who I want to make contact with by asking them whether or not they come from the light.

When using a Ouija board, make sure it is on a flat table. Arrange the sitters holding hands in a circle around the table before starting to build up the energy. Don't allow anyone who has been drinking alcohol or taking drugs to sit at the table, and just have one main communicator asking the questions. Think about the questions before you ask the spirit board what you want to know, and don't ask trivial things such as when somebody is going to die. Everybody should place their hands on the planchette, which slides across the table to different letters in the alphabet to answer the questions. Close down when you are finished and ask any spirit visitors in the room to leave.

**A *word of warning:*** not all spirits are loving beings, as there are confused, mischievous and dark entities out there in the astral that can cause havoc in the home and people's lives if allowed to come in through the use of a Ouija board. If used continually these instruments can cause a possession for the person, home or people involved. You should never use one when you are on your own; there must always be present someone experienced who understands the principles of what they are doing. Dark energy is very active at murder sites and jails or places that have been involved in horrendous crimes. This paranormal activity is harmful but is easy to remove when working with the light, as light energy is more powerful than dark.

## AUTOMATIC WRITING

Automatic writing is one of the oldest forms of divination. By connecting to your heavenly guide or guides, loving messages will easily come from out of nowhere if you practise with an open mind and heart. It is important to do this work at the same time every day when you are first learning how to do it, as it means you are setting up a regular appointment with your loving guides to do this work.

Automatic writing is something I have used and enjoyed for years. I still use it constantly and, when I pray, I often get a pen and paper and am given messages from the spirit world for myself. I have also written books via automatic writing and always get so much information I had no prior knowledge of.

Our spirit guides talk to us all the time, even though we may not be aware of it. Most people unconsciously don't hear the messages they receive just as they sometimes don't listen to what their loved ones are saying! When a thought or message pops up in your consciousness you will often let it go or not take any notice. Your beloved angels or spirit messages are here to guide you throughout life, so take the time to listen and have a bit of faith. When you learn to channel your guides through automatic writing, not only will your world improve but you will join a whole network of other light workers on the planet who are connecting to a higher energy of consciousness and helping Mother Earth become a better place.

To work with automatic writing, sit in a sacred or quiet space where you will not be disturbed and clear the room with white light or burn sage so the energy is clear and clean. I find if I don't do this I pick up other people's problems as I am so sensitive to energy, and it's then harder for me to tune in to my guides. Make yourself comfortable and light a candle. Breathe deeply three times and open yourself up. Place a pen and some paper close by, close your eyes and open your mind to allow whatever wants to come through happen. You can write with your eyes closed but this is not necessary. Write everything down that comes into your mind; don't think about what you are doing. Don't be surprised if you start drawing rather than writing words, as I once did when I was shown a picture of my main guide White Feather in my early spiritual development.

Success will only come with clear intention and dedication to what you want to do. There is no guarantee that automatic writing will work for you straight away but, as with anything, if you persist you will get results. Only ever listen to positive loving messages, which are an indication you are working with light beings that come with a higher intelligence and all that is love. Learn discernment, trust your gut and feel the difference. If in doubt, tell the spirits to leave and go into the light. When you have finished, ask any spirits that are left behind to leave, close down all your chakras and sweep white light through your body.

## DISTANT HEALING

Distant healing is spiritual healing that is applied over distance to the bio-electromagnetic field known as the aura, which contains the blueprint of the physical body. Every single living person or object can receive this energy as it can travel anywhere in the world; you don't have to physically be with the person, pet, plant or situation and it is very effective. The bioplasmic body absorbs life energy and distributes it to the organs and glands. Diseases first appear as energetic disruptions in the energy field before manifesting as ailments in the physical body.

To give a distant or absent healing, find a quiet place in nature or sit in your sacred space where you won't be disturbed. Imagine all of your chakras opening up like little lights and say a prayer if that works for you. Light a candle and place a picture of the person you are healing on your altar. If you don't have a picture, imagine the person or receiver in your mind. Ask the person's higher self if they would like a healing with you; wait to receive the answer. If they say no stop the healing straight away, but continue if they say yes. When you receive a positive reply rub the palms of your hands together and, with your eyes closed, imagine pouring beautiful healing energy and good thoughts of love into your crown chakra down through the body, into your heart and into your hands, sending energy directly into the picture of the person. If you are trained in reiki or any other type of healing you can also send symbols by imagining them being drawn in your mind. When you feel the energy turn off, close down your energy centres and place protection around yourself. You can do this as many times as you feel is required.

# CHAPTER 12

# My spirit team

The best teachers you will have in your development on the spiritual path are your own loving guides and angels. Usually there will be one main guide who stays from birth to death, but other teacher guides and angel helpers will come and go the further you work on yourself and your spiritual practices. We are never alone, not even for a minute. Your guides will work alongside you and then, when you have moved spiritually up to another level or vibration, they may stand back or depart.

While working and studying in different areas on my path I have had many different guides. I fell in love with platform work as I saw how healing it could be on so many levels. I had initially wanted to be an actor and trained at a performing arts school, so I feel that spirit pushed me in the direction I ended up in; I am very confident in front of a camera and large audiences. When I ran my trance classes the sitters could see what my guides looked like through transfiguration and often described their faces.

Guides will come and go as teachers and companions throughout our development. They will chaperone us through difficult times with love, compassion and gentle coaching. The gatekeeper in your mediumship will stay with you from birth to death and is usually someone you have shared a past life with. The rapport you build and the contract you make with your gatekeeper will protect your aura and chakras from unnecessary and inappropriate energies when you are doing light work and will also protect your soul energy. Once you pass into the spirit world and have reviewed how well you did on earth you will be joined by your gatekeeper and soul group.

The following are my own personal spiritual guides, to give you an idea of how they work and the things they can do. It really is quite amazing how much help I get from these wonderful spirit helpers, which I call team spirit. When I ask for it they blend their energies so beautifully.

Guides are an integral part of your mediumship work and will take you to different levels. When I first started I worked with flowers as a psychic link, then I went on to use voice through repeating what I heard. I always work my own guides now, who stand lovingly by my side.

**White Feather, the gatekeeper:** my gatekeeper was introduced to me before I knew I would be working full time as a medium and it became my life's work. While I was meditating one day a gentle voice asked me to draw a picture of an Indian chief with great white feathers in his head. I had once been this great chief's son and we had had a very loving and connected life together.

**Romanov:** a big spirit man with a turban and a beard who worked as a mystic in Ancient Egypt. He is a wise spiritual teacher who shows me how to be strong and use more discernment with people, instead of just rushing in before I really know whom I am dealing with. Romanov told me to only to work with overheads or voice, which I saw as a progression with my mediumship.

**Doctor Lee:** a healing reiki guide who first appeared when I studied and became a reiki master some years ago. He is quite serious, dedicated and very bossy and works with energy and meridians within the body. A small Oriental gentleman with tiny hands who wears his hair in a long plait, he has a restless nature similar to my own and is a curious, intelligent being who likes to get on with the job at hand. When I began doing psychic surgery I was shown and taught many things about the human body through this wonderful guide; I could sense things about people and their diseases and, as soon as I sat down and closed my eyes, healing energy would be channelled from Doctor Lee.

*Margaret:* an older wise woman guide who once worked as a clairvoyant and healer in 18th-century England and who works with flower essences. My interest in vibrational flower essences comes from this loving guide, and I have used these essences since the early 1970s. She taught me how to remove entities from the aura, how to do spirit rescue (or removing lost souls from houses) and how to get rid of spells and curses.

*Three of One:* a delightful and highly intelligent star person or starlight being. He is an unusual tall character of pure light who comes from another dimension. His own planet was destroyed long ago so he lives on spaceships with other light beings that all communicate telepathically to one another through sound waves. Like other beings from different planets, he is helping mankind with the changes we are experiencing on earth. Three of One's interests include teleportation, healing with symbols and teaching people to become empowered and to be more aware of their own abilities.

*Cassandra:* a beautiful, kind, gentle angel whose main concern is helping mankind. The first time I channelled this being I felt very honoured; I couldn't believe such a beautiful being would want to work with me as I can be blunt and don't like to show my softer side to people. This delightful light being has taught me how important it is to honour and love yourself as an eternal soul and to never feel less than others around you. When you learn this simple lesson people will respect you more. Cassandra also believes that taking time out to nurture yourself is critical for your well-being.

*Leon:* my writer guide is quite a character and one of my favourite enlightened beings. He is a practical joker who likes to see the funny side of things. The first time I channelled Leon I could not wipe the smile off my face, as he was so pretentious and snobby and looked like a gay beatnik from the 1950s. He wore tight pants, a polo-neck jumper and a black beanie and had a cigarette hanging out of his mouth. He tells me how important it is to take time out to smell the roses and to stop pushing myself to do things all the time.

*Erin:* a mischievous nature fairy or undine who likes to travel around on the back of birds. Whenever she comes through the room fills with mirth and gaiety. This wise being helps me appreciate nature, as I always feel her around when I am walking in the bush or in my garden. She also helps me with my inner child by teaching me to play and not take life too seriously. Her energy is light and grounding but it can change dramatically as she becomes enraged at the injustice of river and forest pollution. Erin knows a lot about flowers and their energies, and helps me with their use in my vibrational healing practice.

**Red Hawk:** a gentle guide who works with my spirit rescue by helping spirit people lost in the astral to cross over. He is very brave and first stepped forward in my trance group. He looks like a young American Indian as he has long, dark hair and wears simple loin cloths. I felt he was a warrior when alive on the planet as he has paint on his face and a red feather in his hair. He mostly says little and stays very much in the background, but he is happy to give assistance when needed.

**Johnny:** the last to join my team was a young spirit boy who died at a children's hospital at the age of eight. He came to work with me in my closed séances when I started doing Rainbow shows for children and is a real character who loves music, bands and animals.

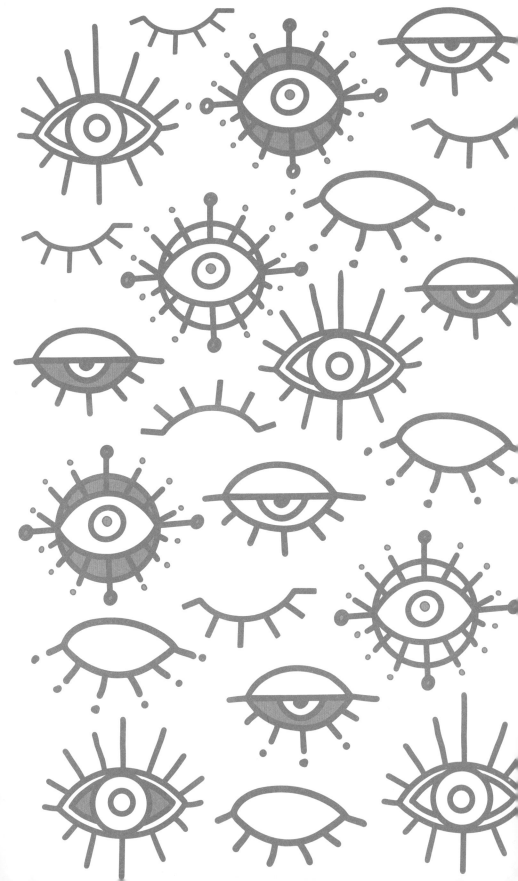

# CHAPTER 13

# Ethics for professional mediums

The following is a list of what you need to know as a professional medium working for the public. Note that the list incorporates things I have learned over the years:

- Always act and dress professionally and communicate well with clear language.
- Be discreet, never discussing information a client gives you with anyone else; confidentiality is paramount.
- Take out adequate insurance and indemnity.
- Undertake proper training, especially when working for the public.

- Don't work if you are unwell, particularly with something contagious such as the flu.
- Never use drugs, chew gum, smoke your head off or drink alcohol in a consultation.
- Protect yourself with white light or whatever ritual you have. I advise my students to say a little prayer before aligning with their guides and spirit people.
- Energetically clear your space when sharing offices or other areas.
- Always close your energies and chakras down after a reading.
- Use protection and ask to work with the client's highest self.
- Never impart negative information, such as when the client or somebody they know is going to die; this is not your right.
- Don't say you can do things that you can't such as banishing a spirit or ridding people of curses for large amounts of money. Unless you are a trained counsellor, if you feel your client needs more help than you can offer pass them on to a trained professional.
- Never call a client to ask them if they want another reading.
- Do not give financial, medical or legal advice, and don't

tell clients what you think they want to hear. Pass on only the information you receive.

❧ Be careful when reading for friends and never read for couples separately, using information about one against the other.

❧ Stop the session immediately if a client appears to have mental problems or be drunk and/or aggressive.

❧ Charge up front. If there is no monetary exchange there is no respect, and unfortunately some people feel they are owed in life and will refuse to pay you.

❧ Always be wary of reading for the media, as some journalists and television hosts will want to ridicule you and will twist your words for the sake of a good story. If you are in a studio just read the audience, not the presenters.

❧ Watch your language and avoid intimacies such as 'hon', 'darling' and 'sweetie'. Show your clients respect by addressing them by their name.

❧ Try not to make your clients your best friends, as it is unprofessional and draining. Maintain boundaries and don't allow clients to make you their private psychic; you are not a charity and your time and energy are important.

❧ Never have a sexual relationship with a client.

- Don't feel sorry for your clients, because in doing this you disempower them.
- Always turn your mobile off before a session, and ensure other people cannot enter the office or room while the session is in progress.
- Never go over time and charge more money unless both parties have agreed to it prior to the session.

## WHAT CLIENTS CAN EXPECT

- If possible use a recommendation from a colleague, friend or family member, as there are many fraudulent mediums among the genuine ones.
- Be wary of gypsies or people who threaten to put a curse on you if you don't pay them an exorbitant amount of money. Report these charlatans to the police as they prey on the vulnerable.
- Your consultation is strictly private and confidential and not to be discussed with anyone else unless you give permission.
- You are entitled to the full and best attention of your consultant. Don't allow other people to enter the session space.

- ⚜ You are entitled to ask questions during the consultation to gain further clarification. By the same token, the medium is allowed to ask questions if it helps to clarify some things during the reading.

- ⚜ You should endeavour to give complete answers to any questions your medium asks; the more open you are the better it will be.

- ⚜ Your consultation is a complete service in itself; you are not required to purchase anything else unless you wish to.

- ⚜ You are entitled to know what your session will cost prior to it happening.

- ⚜ You are completely free to make your own choices. If something that happens in a session doesn't sound right speak up and say so.

- ⚜ If you are not happy with the reading leave in the first 10 minutes or else you will be charged.

- ⚜ Arrive on time for the session as there are likely to be others both before and after yours.

- ⚜ Never abuse the medium; it is unfair to use your consultant as a whipping post or psychiatrist.

# AFTERTHOUGHT

I often imagine life as a constant journey of many changes and different experiences; this is the human experience. It's like we are in a play in which we try out these different roles with each other and ourselves. Often the roles are like a test, repeating themselves until we have finally understood the lesson we were given to learn, whether it be patience, anger, forgiveness, heartache and so on. Some of the experiences can be unpleasant or even stressful and heartbreaking, and take ages to get over if we allow that to happen. Once we perceive what we have created or drawn into our lives to experience we move on, take personal responsibility for ourselves and in reflection ask ourselves what we learned from the experiences and what they taught us. Many of our blocks can be carried through from past lives and continue to repeat themselves

until we have learned to simply move on. This can be done by visiting a professional or healer trained in the specific field, as it is can often be quite difficult to try to do it by yourself.

As I understand it, all healing is about facing our fears or the shadow side of ourselves and surrendering with unconditional love and forgiveness to Great Spirit. I have tried many types of healing, and the most powerful would have to be simple forgiveness on every level. You don't have to actually like the person, but once you have forgiven them you release yourself from the contract, cutting the energy connection that is no longer needed, learning the lesson and moving on to a life of love without fear far better than anything you could ever have believed or imagined . . . because you deserve it.

*'When you follow your path with passion you will blossom like a flower.'*

**Blessings of love and light.**

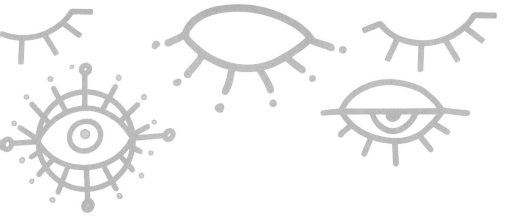

# RECOMMENDED READING

Birch, Silver (2014), *A voice in the wilderness: Teachings from Silver Birch,* White Crow Productions Limited

Brown, Sylvia (2012), *Life on the Other Side: A psychic's tour of the afterlife*, Hatchette UK

Cayce, Edgar (1988), *Edgar Cayce on Dreams*, Grand Central Publishing

Erwin, Kerrie (2019), *Clearing: Your guide to maintaining energy,* Rockpool Publishing

Konstantinos (2004), *Speak with the dead: Seven methods for spirit communication*, Llewellyn Worldwide

Ramadahn (1995), *The Aim of Spirit Revelation Through the Teachings of Ursula Roberts*, Greater World Christian Spiritualist Association

Roberts, Jane (2010), *The Seth Material: The spiritual teacher that launched the new age*, New Awareness Network

Rogers, Rita (2002), *Mysteries*, Pan

Shine, Betty (1990), *Mind to Mind: The secrets of your mind energy revealed*, Random House

Shine, Betty (1994), *Mind Waves: The ultimate energy that could save the world*, Random House

Shine, Betty (2001), *A Free Spirit*, HarperCollins

Smith, Gordon (2007), *Life-changing Messages: Remarkable stories from the other side*, Hay House, Inc.

Stokes, Doris (2000), *A Host of Voices*, Little, Brown

Turoff, Stephen (2007), *Stephen Turoff, Psychic Surgeon: The story of an extraordinary healer*, Thorsons Publishers

Van Praagh, James (1998), *Reading to Heaven: A medium's message of life after death*, Compass Press

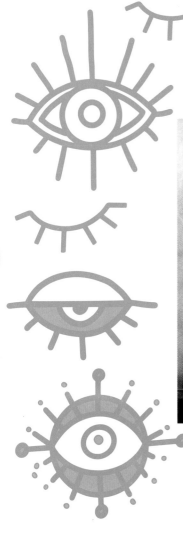